BRAND YOU!
To Land Your Dream Job

A Step-by-Step Guide To Find a Great Job, Get Hired, and Jumpstart Your Career

By
Diane Huth, MA, MBA

San Antonio, TX

BRAND YOU!
To Land Your Dream Job

A Step-by-Step Guide
To Find a Great Job, Get Hired,
and Jumpstart Your Career

By Diane Huth, MA, MBA

Cover Design by Marie Ferrante
Logo Design by Gilda Bejenaru

Inquiries should be addressed to:
Diane Huth
Diane@BrandYouGuide.com
(888) HIREME2

www.BrandYouGuide.com

Published by

ISLA
Publishing Group

ISLA Publishing Group

Printed in the United States of America

ISBN - 13: 978-1541164789
ISBN – 10: 1541164784

TABLE OF CONTENTS

INTRODUCTION

YOUR SECRET WEAPON TO LANDING YOUR DREAM JOB

Finding and landing your ideal job doesn't happen by chance. You have to know the secrets of how to market yourself to land your dream job. You can learn and employ this unique set of skills to ensure you find a good job, get hired, and jumpstart your career. This book will teach you these skills, and share with you an insider's view of what it takes to be the one person out of hundreds of applicants to receive a coveted offer.

In this step-by-step guide, you will discover many valuable insights including how to:

- Use social media to build your personal brand
- Simplify and supercharge your job search with new tools
- Master the hiring process — know what happens when you submit your résumé and job application
- Know what employers look for and reject in a candidate
- Create a powerful résumé
- Write a winning cover letter
- Craft your Elevator Pitch to land a meeting
- Network your way to your dream job
- Access the secret job market where more than half of all jobs are found
- Prepare to ace the interview
- Answer the two key questions that will decide your fate
- Negotiate the highest salary and best benefits

Your dream job is out there somewhere. When you read this book, you will gain the tools and insight to find where it is hidden, get your persuasive credentials into the right hands throughout the hiring process, help you successfully complete the various interviews, and negotiate a great employment package.

The learning here will help you greatly speed up the job-hunting process, furnish you with the tools you will need to succeed, and help you avoid the mistakes and pitfalls that hamper the job search of most people.

So let's get started and get you hired into your dream job!

SECTION 1

SET YOURSELF UP FOR CAREER SUCCESS

Finding the perfect job may seem a daunting challenge in today's difficult employment market. It certainly takes a lot of work, research, networking and creativity to find and land your dream job. But it is achievable with the right information, insights and tools at hand. You've made the first important step in reaching your goal by investing the time and effort to read this book.

In this first section, you will learn how to set yourself up for success when you:

- Realize that there is a light at the end of the tunnel — Chapter 1

- Learn that you are a brand, and that you must market yourself as one — Chapter 2

- Master your online media presence — Chapter 3

- Create your permanent professional name that stands out from the crowd — Chapter 4

- Harness powerful email tools to simplify your search — Chapter 5

- Master correct grammar and spelling to portray a professional image — Chapter 6

1.

Realize That There is a
Light at the End of the Tunnel

Are you frustrated and confused about how to get a job?

Don't know how to network yourself into your dream job?

Discouraged by job board black holes where you send your résumé only to disappear forever?

No clue how to stand out from the crowd to be the one résumé employers pick to interview?

Tired of answering one job post after another with no response?

Haven't a clue how to answer the winner-take-all question — "Tell me about yourself?"

You're not alone. You spend a fortune going to college to learn all sorts of stuff — but no one teaches you the one key skill you really need to know — how to land your dream job and jumpstart your career.

It's a Tough Job Market

The unemployment rate of recent college graduates is double that of the total population, and more than 21% of recent college graduates are either unemployed (7.2%) or underemployed (14.5%.) In 2014, 46% of college graduates worked in jobs that didn't require a college degree. And today, 15% of taxi drivers have a college degree. *Money Magazine* estimates  that it generally takes 3 to 9 months for the average college graduate to get a job. And according to *Newsweek*, millennials make up about 40% of the unemployed.

But don't despair. Of the almost 3 million new graduates to enter the workforce this year, more than 2.2 million of them will find employment. This book will help you to become one of the well-employed professionals, working in a field you love for a good salary.

What Compelled Me to Write This Book

I've worked in brand marketing for what seems like forever – more than 30 years! My career spanned 20 years in top-level marketing slots at a wide range of household-name companies including Johnson & Johnson, Frito-Lay/Sabritas, Carnation/Nestlé, CBS Cable and Mission Foods. I also sold multimedia advertising for 5 years, and held leadership roles with 8 start-up companies.

I am currently Chief Marketing Officer of Biovideo, pioneering maternity photography and videography services, and a Senior Innovation Consultant for Prodigy Works, a national consulting firm.

And in my spare time, I teach Marketing Management, Branding and International Marketing at 2 different universities in Texas.

While teaching marketing students during their final semester of college, I was stunned to find out how poorly prepared they were to search for and land a job.

They didn't understand the dynamics of a job interview, nor how to ferret out the unlisted jobs that go to people in the know without ever being posted on a job board. And none of them knew how to find and meet the people who would hire them. They simply didn't have a clue.

Because I had taught marketing classes at 3 very different universities, I realized lack of preparation wasn't unique to one particular school; it was the same across the board. My students were bright, personable and motivated. But they didn't know how to write a persuasive résumé, prepare a memorable business card, police their social media pages, create a LinkedIn page, or find a mentor. Nor did they know how to network at professional events; and most had never attended professional trade associations where their future employers congregate. They didn't know how to give an elevator pitch, write a cover letter, or ace an interview. And few were prepared to dress for a successful business meeting or interview.

I learned that the Career Services team at each school offered students résumé reviews and help, career seminars, coaching, on-campus job fairs and more — all free to students. But for some reason, few students took advantage of these opportunities. So here they were, just months from graduation, with no concrete plan to get hired into that dream job.

My job was to teach them all about marketing, right? So I developed this program to teach them how to use all the marketing and branding skills they were learning in class to market their most important product — themselves!

First, I taught students in my classes. Then word spread, and I was asked to give the class — which had evolved into a two-hour seminar and then a four-hour workshop — to different classes and student groups on campus. Everywhere, the response was the same: students were amazed to learn precisely what they needed to do to stand out from the crowd and be selected for that one coveted job that so many people were applying for.

I received many requests for the presentation, and realized that just static slides weren't enough. So I decided to write down in detail the many tips and secrets involved in launching and advancing your career so these valuable skills can be learned by anyone anywhere and at any age.

Job Success Secrets for Everyone

This book originally was written for college students getting ready to enter the professional marketplace. But it's not just for students and recent graduates. The insights, tips and recommendations are crucial for any professional in any field, whether just starting out, wanting to change jobs, or being forced to shift gears after an unexpected layoff or life change.

This isn't a static book, something to read and put away. Instead, it's an active guide full of step-by-step assignments to complete, and specific tasks you need to tackle now to get ready to find and land your dream job.

The book is available for college Career Services staff everywhere to help prepare their students to get hired. It's available on Amazon.com and at my live seminars. In addition to the book, you will find valuable information, free templates, useful checklists, and step-by-step tools at no charge at www.BrandYouGuide.com. You will also find lots of additional services and resources to help you prepare to land your dream job.

TIP - Lots of Resources and Links at the End of the Book
At the end of the book, I have summarized all the resources available that I cite throughout the book, along with dozens of links to websites, resources, news articles, government stats, and much more. So don't worry about visiting all the pages while you are reading; they all will be handy in the Resource section at the end.

Keep reading — we're about to find you the job of a lifetime!

2.

Understand That You Are a Brand

You may not realize it but you are a brand. Everything that applies to branding and marketing a product or service applies to marketing yourself. The same principles that I teach in marketing classes apply to branding yourself to land your dream job.

> **"Your personal brand is what people say about you when you leave the room."**
>
> —Jeff Bezos – founder of Amazon

You must create a strong brand name, a persuasive story, and a memorable visual presence; you have to communicate how you will add value, and define and exploit your competitive advantages.

According to Jeff Bezos, the legendary founder of Amazon, "Your personal brand is what people say about you when you leave the room." Your brand is your personal and professional reputation.

It's very important that you take care of your reputation, that you nurture it and that you position it so that what people think and say about you is what you WANT them to think and say.

When you brand yourself properly, the competition becomes irrelevant.

In this book, you will learn how to position and sell yourself so you shine in comparison to the competition and make hiring managers say, "We want THAT person."

➜ TAKEAWAY — In your job search, you should employ many of the same tools and techniques used to market your favorite brands. These will allow you to establish yourself heads and shoulders above everybody else so that employers won't even consider any other candidate for that job. Let's get started!

- Ask everyone you know how they would describe you in just 1 word – and why they chose that word. Perhaps make a game of it and post it on your Facebook, LinkedIn and other social media pages. Copy each word into an Excel spreadsheet and sort by the number of mentions or in alphabetic order. Write down in the second column the number of times each word is mentioned, deduping or deleting multiple mentions. Sort by the highest number of mentions to lowest number of mentions. Then in the third column, indicate whether a potential employer or recruiter would consider that description or trait to be Negative (N) or Positive (P). This is your personal brand. It's a great place to start to figure out how to find and land that great job.

3.

Master Your Online Media Presence

The first step in your job search is to master your social media presence. Think about all the different sites where information about you may appear to a potential employer.

One of the first things any employer or recruiter will do is to look at your social media presence when evaluating you as a potential employee. According to *CareerBuilder*, 51% of companies Google candidates as part of the hiring and selection process. A recent survey by Microsoft found that a whopping 79% of employers now conduct an online search of candidates, and 70% of employers have rejected applicants for what they found online. This is in addition to standard background and reference checks!

So what is your personal brand today?

<u>Google — Start Here First!</u>

Woody Allen once said "80% of success is showing up."

Today, 80% of success is showing up — on Google!

Stop right now and Google your name. That's what any employer is going to do. What does your Google profile show?

- Can you even find yourself?
- Are you on the first page, or on subsequent pages?
- Are there many people with the same name? Or are you unique and listed at the top?
- How many times do you appear, and what is the content of the listings?
- Is there a good photo you want potential employers to see?
- Is there anything negative that you don't want an employer to find?

If you don't have multiple favorable listings ranked right at the top of the search page, with great photos, you have work to do. We will work on establishing your professional name to fix this in Chapter 4.

How to Stand Out on Google Search

Of course you want to show up prominently on Google, and be listed and profiled in a positive manner on Google (and other search engines.) Surprisingly, it's not as hard as you think. Google and all search engines have "spiders" that comb through millions of webpages each month, searching out any published information or stories, and then posting the links, whether you want them to or not. You can't control IF they will post about you — but you can influence WHAT they will post.

If anyone writes a story that's published anywhere and your name is in it, whether it's positive or negative, that story and your name will show up on Google practically forever. So you should proactively strive to secure favorable press coverage that will eventually show up in search engines so these are found first in any search.

One of the best ways to get ranked high in a Google search is to either issue a press release or be mentioned in a release or story. When you issue a press release, you prominently list your name, your phone number, your email address, and sometimes a quote — and all of that will get captured and listed on Google and other search engines.

I served on the Board of the American Marketing Association (AMA) for a number of years and I issued dozens of press releases — that still appear in my Google profile more than 10 years later.

So you should frequently issue a press release for just about anything — your professional association, a club, a social activity, even a church garage sale or a "news article" that you create on your own. This is the easiest way I know to get a favorable first page ranking on Google.

If you don't know how to write a great press release, that's not a problem. We'd be glad to help you get covered by the media.

Find out how at www.BrandYouGuide.com.

TIP — Free Press Release Distribution

While full service press release distribution can cost hundreds of dollars, there are a number of companies that offer free distribution of your press release to a limited online audience. These are great resources, because it doesn't really matter if your release is picked up by anyone except Google! Online releases are often republished by aggregators, so your release may be picked up in strange places — you won't know until you see them on Google! Companies may change their policies over time to eliminate the free release option, but at the time of writing, these companies (and many more) are currently offering free or low cost press release distribution:

- PR.com — http://www.pr.com/

- Online PR News — https://www.onlineprnews.com/

- PressReleaser.org — http://pressreleaser.org/

- Open PR — http://www.openpr.com/news/submit.html

- Google News — http://GoogleNewsSubmit.com/ currently $39

Other ways to be found on Google include a mention in any published newspaper, magazine or trade association article or news report. Write an article for your school paper, or submit a letter to the editor of a magazine or newspaper. Comment on blogs and include your name; perhaps ask to become a guest blogger, or start your own blog. Volunteer, be active at church or professional associations that create or receive media coverage. Another great way to secure coverage is to participate in sporting events that regularly receive some kind of news coverage. So get involved and get noticed.

LinkedIn

One of the first things your prospective employers will do is to look at your LinkedIn page — and see what it says about you professionally. According to one study, 94% of recruiters and human resource (HR) professionals name LinkedIn as the essential source for recruiting. LinkedIn is where you'll build and promote your professional profile, job history, education, affiliations, and so much more. If you don't have a LinkedIn page yet, sign up today. If you have a page already, update it with current information — it will walk you step-by-step through many of the options available. And of course list your contact information, including email and phone number.

A word about your LinkedIn employment profile and résumé: You must be rigorously honest and consistent — no cheating and no exaggeration. Make sure your LinkedIn profile mirrors your résumé. All this information is archived online for anyone to see, and any inconsistencies will pop up instantly. Your online résumé will become a public document that is cached online, so you must be totally honest and upfront about your information. You will learn how to create your powerful résumé in Chapter 14.

LinkedIn is a great networking and self-promotion tool, where colleagues can endorse you for specific skills, and you can show how savvy you are through the number of connections you have. But it can be much more than that. Today you can also post photos, comments, questions, blog posts, skills, presentations, white papers, and more. You can engage with other professionals by answering their questions or responding to and commenting on their posts. This will make you stand out from other job candidates. LinkedIn should be your number one priority in your job search.

Basic LinkedIn services are free, and a basic account generally is adequate if you are employed. But if you are actively seeking a new job, you might consider upgrading to a Premium account which gives you access to hidden profiles and the ability to send InMail directly to any LinkedIn member. LinkedIn has recently introduced the Career Plan, tailored for job seekers, at $29.99 per month. It may well be worth the investment if it helps you land your next job. LinkedIn is a powerful tool to network and reach out to potential employers or business colleagues you wouldn't be able to reach otherwise.

If you'd like help polishing your LinkedIn profile, feel free to contact me at BrandYouGuide.com.

TIP — LinkedIn Etiquette — Gaining Endorsements
You want people to endorse you for your skills, especially as you start out your career. The easiest way is to endorse them first! Just review all your contacts and write a short but glowing endorsement about each of them — a sentence or two is enough — and submit in online. In return, the majority will give YOU an endorsement. And you don't even have to ask them for it!

➡ TAKEAWAY — LinkedIn is your # 1 social media network when job hunting. Create and maintain a great LinkedIn page, and actively use it to promote yourself using its many tools.

Facebook

Half of all potential employers will look at your Facebook page as part of the screening process, according to *CareerBuilder*. It will tell them who you are as a person — what your interests are, how you spend your time, who you associate with, how you express yourself in writing, your political affiliation, whether or not you are married, or if you are a partier, a jock or a couch potato. What are they going to find on YOUR Facebook page today?

Search through the last 3 months of your Facebook posts and evaluate yourself as an employer will. Are you family-oriented, or do you hang out with friends? Do you drink and go to nightclubs and party hard every weekend? Do you spend hours on end playing video games? What values do you express in your posts? Are many of your posts about alcohol, sex or laced with profanity or cynicism? Or do you engage in positive or altruistic activities such as volunteer work or church activities? Do you walk in charity events, belong to the Y, or participate in Ironman competitions? Do you care for and spend time with parents, family members, your spouse or children? Potential employers will look at your posts with these questions in mind to understand you as a person.

You should also stay clear of political posts and comments on your Facebook page. Half of all Americans belong to the other party, so you can't afford to offend them!

Employers are generally looking for a stable mature adult with some family responsibilities so they know you will take the job seriously and won't quit on a whim. Any potential employer will invest tens of thousands of dollars in training you for the job, and they want to feel comfortable that you are a reliable, serious employee who will fit into the company culture.

3 Steps to Manage Your Facebook Postings

1. Go through your own Facebook timeline and delete any photos or posts that will not look good to a potential employer. To remove objectionable posts, highlight the little down arrow on the top right corner of the post, and click "delete" or "hide from timeline."
2. If you are tagged in someone else's unflattering post, ask them to hide or delete the post in which you are tagged.
3. Actively start posting positive messages and images that a potential employer will appreciate. Post inspirational messages. Talk about positive things you are doing. Post about successes in school or work, or charity events you are involved in. Make posts that show your value system. Post about family members and business or community leaders you admire. Share positive stats, information, or images relating to your profession. But

be authentic. Let your Facebook page sing your praises to a potential employer.

TIP — Google Might Find That Photo!
Beware of photos that show you in a less-than-desirable pose. Does your Facebook page show a photo of you partying drunk on Spring Break, or dressed provocatively, or making an obscene gesture? Google's spiders search through images on the Web, and they could pick up unflattering photos of you to post on Google Images! If they do, it might be very hard to make these go away. So be aware that everything that's on social media may be visible to a potential employer.

➔ TAKEAWAY — Have a professional Facebook page available for potential employers to easily find. If you aren't willing to have a single page that meets both your personal and professional needs, then you should consider making your current personal page private, and creating a separate public Facebook page in your full professional name that you will use on your résumé (more on that in Chapter 4.)

Twitter

Do you Tweet? Prospective employers may look at your Twitter feed and see what you're talking about. They're going to see if your posts are insightful or silly, if you follow thoughtful leaders and journalists or shallow Hollywood celebrities, and so much more. Use Twitter to showcase your skills and strengths, not to show weaknesses.

Use Twitter to Grow Professionally and Impress Prospective Employers

Most people think of using Twitter for fun, but it can play a very important role in your career. Most journalists use Twitter to post their stories and interact with followers.   Follow a dozen or so important thought leaders in your desired industry, and comment insightfully every time they post a new story. You will go far in your own professional networking, and you will impress potential employers with your commitment to and knowledge of your field.

TIP — Twitter is Important for Marketers and Many Business Fields

You will need to have a Twitter account if you work in marketing, journalism, public relations, and many other fields. If you want to get a story published, you need to follow the key writers you wish to engage with through their Twitter feeds. For example, if you want to place a story in *Forbes*, follow the writers and editors who cover your industry or topics for *Forbes*. Start following them on Twitter, LIKE and SHARE their stories, and post insightful and favorable comments on every story. Soon you will be chatting with key writers like old friends, so when you want to place a story in *Forbes*, you have a colleague that you can easily contact.

Additional Social Media Pages and Tools You May Need

While LinkedIn, Facebook, and Twitter are the top social media sites you will need for your job search, you can use several other social media and digital tools for promoting your professional life. Take a few moments now to register these accounts in your same professional name so you have a consistent social media presence.

Pinterest

You should have a professional Pinterest page — it's not just for women and personal fun anymore. Create a professional account with boards that profile your professional heroes, give motivational quotes, state key insights about your profession, etc. LIKE each pin you post, then follow everyone whose pin you post, and they will probably follow you — allowing you to build your social media following. You can even link your Pinterest page directly to your Facebook page or Twitter account, and share pins directly to those social media sites.

Google+

I personally don't use Google+, but many business professionals do. The key benefits include immediate listing of your content on Google, and a higher Google ranking for your page and content than through organic search. If you register a YouTube page, you will automatically be assigned a Google+ page. To put it in perspective, there are more active Google+ accounts than Twitter accounts, so you understand the scale it offers. With the growing power of Google, I suggest that you register a Google+ page in your name now, even if you don't do anything with it right now. Or just duplicate your Facebook or LinkedIn posts on G+ using HootSuite.

YouTube

 Communication today is shifting to video, so take the time now to register your own professional YouTube channel. You don't even need to post anything on your own channel today to benefit your job search. Simply subscribe to the channel of every company or brand you want to work for — and their competitors. For example, if you want to work for Procter and Gamble (P&G) on Pampers, subscribe to Pampers' YouTube Channel, and also to Huggies' and LUV's channels. Every time one of them posts a new video, you'll get an email alert so you can immediately watch the video. You can LIKE it, SHARE it, and post comments on the page that will be seen by Pampers' marketing team. You can send an email commenting on the new video to the recruiter or hiring manager at P&G that you want to connect with. At your upcoming job interview, you can say "I found your new Olympics video campaign was very motivational and right on target," or make an insightful comment about a competitor's campaign. Are you going to look sharp or what?

Even if you don't use your professional page now, you will have your name reserved for use in the future. Post your holiday vacation videos on a *personal* page; create and use your *professional* page for the many professional videos you will make as you evolve in your career.

Register New Social Media Pages as They Become Popular

 Social media pages are free to claim and register today, so you might as well grab them while you can to secure them in your name. Why let somebody else take your name? Sometime in the next ten years, you may need these and other new social media sites. So register all your professional social media pages — including Instagram and Snap Chat and other new social media accounts as they become popular.

Other Online Marketing Tools to Claim Now

 While you're at it, you may want to secure a free Skype account for free video calls anywhere in the world, regardless of your cellular carrier. Some companies also use Skype for video interviews.

 You can also register for an easy-to-use Mail Chimp account — it's free for the first 2,000 emails in your database, for unlimited email deliveries each month — that is a huge number of contacts.

 You might as well register for a free EventBrite account at the same time, which will allow you to easily plan and promote events for free.

22

With these social media tools, you will be well on your way to a powerful personal branding program using cutting edge digital techniques.

The Easy Way to Find and Register Your Social Media Pages

A key to building your online presence is to have multiple social media pages. When I set up my Superhero Branding program, I spent hours searching and registering all the different social media sites I thought I might need in the future.

Then I learned that there's a much better way. I have found two companies, KnowEm.com and Namech_k.com, that will actually search all the social media sites and tell you if your name is available on each different page. It can save you hours of time.

How to Manage Your Social Media Accounts and Posts

 HootSuite is a great free tool for managing all your social media accounts. The basic membership is free, and there is a small monthly fee for multiple users on one account for businesses. You can quickly and easily schedule your posts across multiple social media pages — Facebook, Twitter, LinkedIn, Google+, WordPress, Instagram and YouTube. This is an effective way to be professionally active in social media without driving yourself crazy!

Buy Your Own Domain Name and Create Your Own Website

Now is the time to register your own professional name as a domain name before anyone else does. I bought www.DianeHuth.com more than a decade ago. I don't do anything with it because I'm busy with other things and have it redirected to one of my business websites, but I would never give it up so someone else could take it.

I strongly recommend you use GoDaddy for all your domain and web services — I have had nothing but the most outstanding customer service from them 24/7 by knowledgeable techs who live in the United States! They are the only web domain and web services company you ever will need. It'll cost you around $20 a year to own your domain name. They often offer discounts for services — right now they are offering a promotion for $1.00 for a new annual domain registration, $1.00 per month Website Builder and $3.99 per month web hosting with professional emails.

I suggest you build a small 1- to 3-page professional website to serve as a digital résumé and portfolio. Showcase your skills, projects you have done, your business philosophy and more. The GoDaddy Website Builder is very easy and intuitive to use, and you can build a professional and attractive website in just a few hours. Then it just takes minutes to update it at no additional cost. If you need help building your site, contact us at Help@BrandYouGuide.com.

Start Your Own Consulting Company

I believe that as a professional, you should have your own consulting company, to serve as credentials when unemployed or looking or a job, and to be a Plan B in your career. You don't have to do anything other than print business cards and build a small website that you are planning to do anyway, right? You don't need to file for an LLC or incorporate if you use your own name and work as a sole proprietorship. You may want to apply for a Fictitious Name for your business if you choose a name other than your own name. Check out the page on Corporations on your local state Secretary of State webpage for rules on sole proprietorships and taxation as these vary state-to-state.

One important benefit is that you can interface with potential employers as a professional peer rather than as a job applicant. As a consultant, you are able to reach out to the hiring manager, while as a job seeker, the organization tries to limit contact through the HR department.

You can do volunteer work through your company, and list them as clients. And there are great tax benefits for working out of a home office.

Monitor Your Credit Report

Today, about 35% of companies use your credit report to find out how responsible you are and to judge your character. When you sign the job application, you give the employer permission to access personal information, which includes your credit report. If you have a poor or average credit score, work to improve it now by paying down balances, and ensuring you pay minimum balances on time. If you are new to the work market, you may not have a credit rating. In this case, apply for 3 or 4 credit cards (Master Card, Visa, retail cards, gas cards, etc.), use each of these at least once a month, and pay them off promptly each month. This will help build a high credit score quickly. Several major credit cards (including Capital One, Chase and Bank of America) offer free credit reports as a feature of their card app. Check your credit score monthly to track your credit-building progress.

Keep Track of all Your Social Media and Digital Media Accounts

You will need to keep track of all your domain names and social media pages, or the constantly changing passwords will drive you crazy. I create a spreadsheet and record all my domain names, account numbers, social media pages, login email addresses, passwords, date of last update and more. You might even want to keep it in a Cloud drive to access from anywhere when you are away from your primary computer. This is in addition to my Password Manager app below.

Managing Your Passwords

I recommend you use a Password Manager program to keep track of all your passwords and log in information for all your accounts. I use Dashlane with an annual premium subscription costing around $40 per year. It automatically records each domain and account, and the login information, and then syncs across all platforms. According to *PC World*, the top ranked password managers include Dashlane, Sticky Password and Last Pass at the time this book was written. I suggest you do a Google search for "Best Password Managers" to select one that meets your needs.

TIP — Create Easy-to-Remember Passwords
You will be required to update your password frequently for many social media accounts. Instead of creating new passwords each time, you can change these by adding a progressive letter behind your standard password — which is much easier to remember. Example — Pass13*a, Pass13*b, Pass13*c, etc. I tend to create an 8-digit password with a combination of caps, low case letters, numbers and special characters so it will work on the vast majority of sites. Then I just change the last character sequentially from A up to Z so the password is easy to remember and recover.

Monitor and Track Your Social Media Brand Presence

Monitoring, tracking and updating your social media presence is an ongoing responsibility. Set aside a block of time each week or month to update your LinkedIn page and monitor all of your social media accounts. This is an ongoing responsibility — to monitor, track and enhance your social media presence.

Google Yourself Monthly

Make yourself a calendar alert for once a month to conduct a Google search of your own name. Take a screen shot of the home page and any other pages you appear on; date it and keep it in a file. Over time you will be able to see changes as your brand presence increases.

Set Google Alerts

Here's a handy secret tool you may not know about. Go to Google Alerts and set up a free account to track anything published about yourself, your industry, your school or university, potential employers, even topics you are interested in. You can register up to 10 free names, keywords, or domain names. You will receive an email whenever your listed name or keyword is mentioned in any media or online post anywhere. So if you've sent those press releases and one gets picked up in an online blog anywhere in the country, you will learn about it instantly! Armed with this hot-off-the-presses information, you can proactively reach out to prospective employers and mentors immediately, mentioning the content of the news story, so they know you are really connected, alert, and on the cutting edge — just the kind of employee they are looking for!

➔ TAKEAWAY — In today's market, you must be savvy with social media and digital tools to be successful in your job hunt. Learn to manage all your social media pages knowing that any potential employer or recruiter will check them out early in the screening process. Tap into the power of sites like LinkedIn to showcase your skills and talents in a positive manner.

To Do List

- Google yourself! Take a screen shot and save. Re-do monthly, save and compare.

- Distribute a press release with your name and contact name in it — periodically.

- Review your Facebook and Twitter pages and delete anything you don't want a recruiter or a future boss to see.

- Build a complete and professional LinkedIn page; find people you know and endorse them. Write a short but glowing testimonial of those you know well.

- Claim your name on key social media pages — Facebook, Twitter, Google+, Pinterest YouTube, Instagram, Snapchat, and others that may arise in popularity. You don't need to build pages for all of them, but reserve your name

- Register for a free account with key marketing tools you may need in the future — Skype, Mail Chimp, EventBrite, HootSuite, etc.

- Purchase your domain name at GoDaddy, and build a simple 1 to 3-page personal website to show your credentials and portfolio.

- Run a free credit report, and repeat every 3 months. Copy and save in a file to compare progress. Pay off credit cards, get more credit cards, and actively manage your credit report.

- Set Google Alerts for your name and the companies you want to work for.

4.

Select Your Professional Name
— and Stick with it Forever

You need to select the professional name that you'll use forever. Your professional name will appear on your résumé, LinkedIn page, personal or professional website, permanent email address, business cards, diplomas, transcripts, and more.

When you did your Google search, how many people were listed with the same name as yours? If just one or two, then you don't have a problem — other than having a very strange or unusual name!

Most likely, there were dozens of people with the same name. So you need to create your permanent name to be as distinctive yet professional as possible to stand out in social media and avoid confusion with someone with a similar name.

Most names are fairly common, so you will probably want to add a middle initial or middle name — which will allow you to stand out. Some people don't have a middle name. If that is the case, just make one up — you get to choose! How fun! But make up one that you will like, because you will be stuck with it for a long time. You could choose an unusual middle initial — Q, X, Y and Z are all good — that will probably be unique as well.

You should also avoid fun or frivolous nicknames that might not be considered adequately professional. This is not the time to add your nickname of Bambi, Baby, Bonzo or Rocketman — leave those nicknames for close friends and family only and for your personal email.

For Women Only — Should You Use Your Maiden or Married Name?

If you are an unmarried woman, you should use your first, middle and last name. When you marry, I suggest that you replace your middle name with your maiden name, and then add your husband's name as your last name. For example, my maiden name was Diane Margaret Clauss, but when I married I dropped Margaret and added Huth — so my name now is Diane Clauss Huth.

When I divorced, I decided not to change my name back to my maiden name, because by that time I had established it as my professional name and it's my son's last name. However, if I had decided to drop my ex-husband's last name, most people would have been able to find me through my maiden name which I had kept as part of my legal married name.

Recommendations for Managing Married and Maiden Names

- **If you are young and plan to have children**, it will be easier on everyone involved if you adopt your husband's last name. Otherwise, your children's last names will be different from your name, which is very confusing to everyone, especially teachers and administrators. Plus, you will receive letters and Christmas cards addressed to Mr. and Mrs., and it just becomes a hassle. The wife of a cousin of mine refused to take his last name, and she spent decades scolding everyone about the Mr. & Mrs. issue, which only served to alienate everyone involved. It was a waste of time, effort and goodwill.

- **If you are a mature professional and you already have children**, you might want to keep your married name if you divorce. It will be much easier on everyone involved, and much simpler for the kids. Your professional name is your brand equity, and it is risky to change your personal branding unless absolutely necessary.

- **If your ex was Attila the Hun** and you absolutely hate him and his name, then by all means change it back to your maiden name. But beware that it will take time and effort to make the change to government documents, passports, drivers' licenses, diplomas and transcripts, social media pages, medical insurance, ID cards, mortgages, banks, and more.

- **Avoid hyphenating your husband's name** after your last name. A few years ago, it was popular for Mary Ellen Jones to become Mary Ellen Jones-Smith when she married Mr. Smith. But that just doesn't work for many government and industry online forms. For example, when traveling internationally, the customs agents will look at your last name only, so you will be registered as Smith or Jones and not Jones-Smith, which will drive computers crazy and may not match your passport. In addition, your hyphenated last name may be too long for certain forms or computer applications and you might end up being listed as Mary Ellen Jones-Sm. That doesn't work well either.

- **All this is easy to do** — just declare your new married name when you fill out the marriage certificate and send in your change of name to Social Security. Same thing when you get a divorce — just declare what your name will be. No need to go to court to make a name change or do any special legal filing.

➜ TAKEAWAY — Now is the time to select and adopt a distinctive professional name and apply it consistently throughout your job search and professional life. Women, decide your long-term naming strategy now, and stick with it.

- Google your name to see how far down in the Google ranking it appears.

- Select a professional name that is distinctive from all others that come ranked before yours. You might use a middle initial or middle name to make sure your name is distinctive.

- Ladies, determine how you will handle the maiden name issue when you marry.

- Make sure you use only that official name in everything you do — driver's license, college transcripts, LinkedIn page, resume, email address, and more.

5.

Harness Powerful Email Tools
for Your Job Search

Create a Professional Gmail Account

 A professional email address in your professional name is crucial for your personal branding. According to the website *BeHiring.com*, using an unprofessional email address will cause you to be rejected 76% of the time!

Not using Gmail yet? I strongly suggest that you create a Gmail account for your professional name. Gmail provides you with a wide range of apps and add-ons that will make your job search so much easier and efficient.

Hopefully, you can get your professional name@gmail.com account without a problem. But if it is already taken, try using hyphens or periods to create your unique Gmail account.

For example, my professional email account is DianeHuth@gmail.com. But if it wasn't available, I could have tried one of these alternative addresses: Diane.Huth or Diane.C.Huth, or Diane-Huth or even DianeHuthTX. With email addresses, caps and low case letters are interchangeable — it doesn't matter which you use. So you can use caps in promoting or listing your email address for good readability and to correspond to your name visually. The key is to keep the name integrity to ensure your email address is easily memorable and identifiable as being you.

TIP — Gmail is Wonderful!
You'll use Gmail for everything. It links to the whole Google ecosystem, so claim your name before someone else does. For older professionals, legacy email accounts like AOL, Yahoo, and People PC are considered old fashioned and may indicate that you are older and/or not up to date with your social media skills. Similarly, avoid using email addresses from your internet or cable company. When you change service or move, you may have to give up that address, which will seriously hamper your personal branding program.

If you set up your own website and domain name, you may be able to use a permanent email address like diane@dianehuth.com. For $50 a year, Gmail can also administer your email account so you can access all the other great marketing tools that integrate with the Google platform.

Create a Visual Signature Stamp

As you communicate with potential employers — and for the rest of your life — you need a professional graphic signature. Google has a free app called WiseStamp (https://Webapp.wisestamp.com/) that will create a signature as a picture that looks like this:

Diane Huth
Marketing Meister, Superhero Branding
(210) 601-7852 || Diane@SuperheroBranding.com ||
https://www.SuperheroBranding.com || Skype: diane huth

It can feature your picture, email, phone, website, social media pages, and more. For less than $50 per year, you can upgrade to a pro account with multiple signatures customized to different email accounts and extra add-ons.

So instead of just typing your name and contact info when you are corresponding with a potential employer, you can brand yourself with a visual WiseStamp signature.

Set Up Email Tracking

Since you will be using email to reach prospective employers, you can benefit from setting up Email Tracking to know who and when someone opened your emails. A number of different services offer detailed tracking for your Gmail account, notifying you when someone opens your email, how many times it is opened, for how long it is open, and if it is forwarded and to whom. A tracking program ranges from free for a limited number of emails per day to unlimited emails for around $10 per month. *Computer World* in 2015 rated Bananatag, Boomerang, Mail2Cloud, MailTrack, Sidekick and YesWare as the best mail tracking programs.

To Do List

- Sign up for a Gmail account in your professional name.

- Create a visual signature stamp.

- Set up email tracking to see when your emails are opened.

6.

Master Correct Grammar and Spelling

In everything you do in your professional branding, you must be rigorous about grammar and spelling. There is no room for typos, misspelling, incorrect word usage, profanity, poor formatting, run-on sentences, or sloppy or unprofessional presentation.

According to *CareerBuilder.com*, 61% of recruiters will reject your résumé if it contains a single typo. And 43% of hiring managers will do the same thing, according to Adecco, a leading employment agency.

If I see a résumé, cover letter or LinkedIn profile that has a typo, bad grammar, or misspelling, I think that the candidate is not good enough to work for me. I immediately discard that résumé or application and go on to the next candidate. If something as important as your job-hunting materials aren't perfect, and if you don't carefully proofread, and you can't get the spelling and grammar right, I expect your work to be equally sloppy and unprofessional. I won't spend time teaching you how to spell or write as an employee. You have to get it right always.

<u>Run All Communication Through a Spelling and Grammar Checker</u>

Microsoft Word makes it incredibly simple to check your documents for errors, typos and bad grammar. It should automatically underscore in red any misspellings. But just in case, run a spelling and grammar check when you finish drafting a document of any kind, including a preliminary draft of an email before you copy it into your word processing program. In the top menu bar, click Review, then Spelling & Grammar and it will take you  through every questionable item in the document for you to accept or change. Make a habit of checking all key documents before sending them. It can make the difference between getting the job or getting rejected – it is that important.

<u>Tools for Improving Your Communication</u>

If you don't have perfect English grammar and spelling, work on it immediately, as it will be a key barrier to getting a good job. If you are in school, you may be able to get a tutor from Career Services.
Always have your résumé and cover letter template reviewed by one or more people with great grammar.

Also avoid industry jargon and abbreviations whenever possible to ensure all recipients can understand what you are trying to say.

The easiest way to actively improve your grammar and word choice is to download and practice with any of dozens of great mobile apps that will train you on correct grammar. Here is a short list of some highly-recommended mobile apps that are free or inexpensive: Grammaropolis Complete, English Grammar Book, Grammar Up, Grammar Girl App, Grammar Phone, Grammar Police, Grammar Guru, Grammar App, and Practice English Grammar.

In addition, there is an app — <u>Grammarly.com</u> — that will check all of your emails before you send them. It works on both your emails and Word documents, and will send you a weekly report of key errors you tend to make to help you correct your grammar.

- Always check your documents and emails thoroughly for grammar and spelling errors

- Use Word's Spelling and Grammar Check tool whenever possible

- Get tutoring if this is a challenge for you — it will impact your career

- Download one or more grammar apps and practice with them daily

Now that you've established your digital and online presence, you are one step closer to finding your dream job. But, you still have more work to do. Next you need to gather real-life tools for your job search.

SECTION 2

GATHER ALL THE TOOLS FOR YOUR JOB SEARCH

Before starting your job search, you need to arm yourself with all the tools to launch a successful effort. Don't waste your time and potential employers' interest by being unprepared. You only have one chance to make a good impression, so invest the time now to thoroughly create or gather the resources that will make this process easier and more likely to result in getting hired.

In this section, you will learn how to:

- Find your career passion — Chapter 7
- Use a professional photo to makes all the difference — Chapter 8
- Create and print a professional business card — Chapter 9
- Identify who really makes the hiring decision — Chapter 10
- Find and recruit mentors — Chapter 11
- Line up your personal and professional references — Chapter 12
- Get an internship — the # 1 way to land your dream job — Chapter 13
- Create a powerful and engaging résumé — Chapter 14
- Cold call using a Broadcast Letter instead of a résumé — Chapter 15

7.

Find Your Passion

Before you seriously embark on your job search, you need to know what you want in a job, and why.

I know you want to get out of school and land a job that pays well and offers good benefits. You may want to buy a new car, travel, buy a home or pursue your other plans and dreams. But you *need* to figure out a little bit more than that.

I hate to tell you this, but you're going to work until you are almost 70 years old — if you are a recent graduate or still in school. That means you're going to work for 40 to 50 years in total. Can you imagine that?

Retirement age today is 67 for Social Security. It's going to be almost 70 by the time today's grads age into Social Security. So it's critical that you find a profession that you like and enjoy enough that you can comfortably do it for 30 to 40 years. The good news is, Marketing is one of those professions, in my experience, and it has kept me stimulated and interested for more than 35 years — that's pretty amazing. It's right for me, but maybe not for you.

You need to ask yourself, "What do I love to do?" Write it down, "I love to _____." List lots of things you love to do, and rank them by your preference.

 Then ask yourself, "What am I really, really, really good at?" What you love and what you are good at may not be the same things. Often the two are the same, because you tend to love to do what you're competent at, and you hone your skills doing things you love, but not always.

Then, you need to figure out what someone will pay you to do. What skills are involved in what you love to do and what you are good at? Identify marketable skills that are in demand, and careers or jobs that require someone with your unique skills so you can command a decent salary.

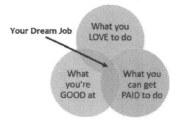

39

essional Passion Matrix

tor John Highland uses what I call the Professional Passion
out the right career path. He developed this process when
ultant at McKinsey, a leading consulting firm, and has used
nterviewing job candidates.

Ask ·ᴜ·   ᐧ Questions — Right Now — And Write Down the Answers:

1. What do you do BEST?

_____

_____

2. What do you LOVE to do?

_____

_____

3. What are your key WEAKNESSES?

_____

_____

4. What do you HATE to do?

_____

_____

Making Sense of the Answers

1. **What you do BEST** is what you should be doing because it is your key strength. It is the tangible set of skills you offer your employer. This is the easiest job to find right now because you can demonstrate expertise and mastery. It should pay your bills today.

2. **What you LOVE to do** is your future. It's where you should strive to be long term. Look for jobs that allow you to grow into that dream job. Work on gaining the skills and experiences to move into that position as soon as

possible. Take online courses, go back to school, study for a certification, join a trade association, or network with other professionals in the field.

The Personal Passions Matrix

What do you do BEST? This is what you should be doing now.	What do you LOVE to do? This is your future.
What are your key WEAKNESSES? Work to master these skills.	What do you HATE to do? Avoid this at all costs.

3. **Your WEAKNESSES** are what may keep you from attaining your goal. First, determine whether or not these are critical to success in your field and future career. Focus on more relevant weaknesses first. For example, if you are an accountant, and public speaking is your weakness, it probably is not a deal breaker. However, if you work in marketing or sales, it may be detrimental to your success. So if you determine that these weaknesses ARE critical to your success, you need to take action immediately to improve your skills, and hopefully to gain expertise in the field. Get a tutor, sign up for classes, get a life coach, take online courses, go to a workshop or seminar, and then practice the skill set until you reach an acceptable level. In the case of the person seeking a marketing job, that might mean joining Toastmasters for public speaking experience, taking an acting or debate class or seminar, reading books on public speaking techniques to gain a better sense of comfort and control, and more.

4. **Avoid doing what you HATE.** There is no reason to make yourself miserable by taking a job that you will hate every day. Remember, you will be working professionally for 30 or 40 years or more, and you don't want that time to be drudgery. In addition, you will probably do poorly at any job you really hate. You will be a failure at that job, and hate it even more. For example, I really hate cold calling and direct sales, especially telephone sales. It gives me a knot in my stomach, and makes me nervous and anxious and irritable. So I avoid getting around to making those awful sales calls until it's the end of the day and too late to do anything. Sometimes I'll just make busywork to avoid making the calls at all. I don't do it well, and I am miserable. It's not the right job for me. Other people love direct sales, relish

the challenge, wake up excited to get to work to start calling on new customers. That's the right job for them. So find a job you really enjoy; you will be happier. And your company will be more successful and profitable.

Find Your Professional Passion Before Embarking on Your Job Search

Take the time now for some real soul searching so you can embark on the right career path. Here are ways to help you find your passion:

- Talk with people in the field you are considering to make sure the work fits your interests and temperament.
- Find someone in that field, and ask for half an hour of their time to pick their brain at work, or offer to buy them coffee after work or treat them to a working lunch near their office.
- Work with a career coach or counselor if possible.
- Find out what vocational testing and coaching you can get for free from your state unemployment or job services office — they may be able to help you figure out your skills and aptitudes.
- Go to your Career Services office at school and ask for help.
- If you are still in school, by all means take one or more internships in your desired field to make certain that it is the right choice for you.
- Invest in vocational testing.
- Job shadow someone at work for a day to see the reality of the job. This would probably require HR's permission at a big company, but would be doable for a small company.

What If You Really Don't Know What You Want to Do?

One of the purposes of 4 years of college is to expose yourself to the many different aspects of life and work so you will have a better chance of finding your passion. But many people just don't find it there. Remember, as a professional, you should really enjoy your work, not hate it. You should wake up excited to get started on a new project or brainstorm ideas with a colleague. Ideally, work should be interesting, stimulating and personally rewarding at many levels. So work hard on figuring out what your passions are to get your career on track.

If you absolutely don't have anything you want to do, I highly recommend that you register with a temporary services agency and take a number of different assignments, which will expose you to many different companies, managers and fields. This is a great way to figure out what you want to do, and what company you want to work for. Often employers who love you will offer to keep you on as a direct employee after the contract period expires.

If that doesn't work, then perhaps you should take a break and do something far out of your comfort zone and field of expertise. Take a job as a waiter or ride-share driver or a construction worker or a retail sales clerk to help define what you do and don't like. Driving a forklift in a warehouse or garnishing dinner platters at a restaurant (which my son Alex did while going to school) will make you remember why you went to school in the first place. Maybe you'll love it or maybe you'll hate it, but you'll be one step closer to finding your passion.

Don't Change Jobs Too Often

Don't just take a job because you don't have anything else better, and then quit when you aren't happy there. Frequent job changing (more frequent than every 2 years!) is seriously frowned upon by employers, and causes you to be seen as an unreliable employee.

When you are employed in a professional capacity, your employer will invest thousands of dollars in training you. That includes your salary and benefits during training time when you aren't producing anything at work, the cost of your trainer or coach, travel expenses to a training meeting or conference, and more. So they won't take a risk and hire you if they think you won't stay around long.

The best possible thing on your résumé is a steady job for 2+ years while in school. This will demonstrate that you are serious, committed, reliable, and hard working. It doesn't matter if the job was to clerk at a store, nanny for small children, stock grocery shelves at night, or sell tickets at the movie theater. The demonstration of RELIABILITY is the important factor.

If you changed jobs frequently, you need a clear and persuasive explanation about the job churning. Acceptable reasons include:

- The company was sold or closed
- The company had an RIF (Reduction in Force)
- You are married to a soldier who was reassigned
- You moved for family reasons
- The job was seasonal
- You had to change schools to finish your degree
- You had to leave due to school demands (couldn't accommodate your work schedule and you needed to take day classes to finish your degree program, for example)

But whatever the reason you churned jobs, don't give negative reasons for leaving like:

- I didn't like my boss
- The work was boring
- I obtained a better job
- It didn't pay enough

- They wouldn't let me take vacation when I wanted it
- I didn't like the people I worked with
- It was too long of a drive to work

➜ TAKEAWAY — Invest the time right now to do a great deal of soul searching, discussion, counseling, even personality testing to figure out what job will satisfy you for years to come. When you know what you really want to do, your job search will become much more targeted and efficient and effective. Don't waste your time applying for jobs that you won't love.

- Invest the energy now to find out what you really want to do professionally.

- Consider vocational testing at school or on you own to help give you insights into your personality and the kinds of fields that statistically might be interesting to you — many you might not have thought of before.

- Complete the Professional Passions Matrix to help figure out what your love to do and are best at.

- Make a list of all the jobs you think you would love. Close your eyes and imagine yourself in that career. Then make a list of all the jobs you would hate to do. Compare them to see if you can learn from that exercise.

- If you really don't know what you want to do professionally, sign up for a temp services company and work in lots of different fields for many different companies. It should help you better identify what you like and don't like to do.

- Consider taking an off-the-wall job in some completely different field to help provide clarity.

8.

Take a Professional Photo
For All Your Job-Hunting Needs

Every great brand needs to have a great logo or image — and so do you. In your case, it is a professional studio photo that you will use everywhere as you brand yourself — on business cards, on your LinkedIn page, press releases, personal website, volunteer positions and more.

According to research by *TheLadders.com*, 19% of a recruiter's time on your LinkedIn page is spent viewing your photo. Let your photo clearly state, "I am a competent, well-groomed professional, who dresses in professional business attire.

What to Wear

Men should wear a navy blue, dark blue, dark grey, charcoal gray, or black suit, with a fine silk power tie, preferably red, blue, solid colors, or thin stripes or a fine pattern that ties the shirt and suit together. Wear a crisp white freshly-ironed long sleeved shirt.

Women should wear a professional long sleeved suit in a solid color with a white or solid colored blouse, accented by tasteful gold, silver or pearl jewelry.

Both men and women will need a basic navy blue suit for work, so you might as well get one now. This is the suit you will wear on your job interview, so invest in at least one quality suit now. It doesn't need to be an expensive designer suit, but it does need to be well-cut, of quality fabric, with fine stitching, and fit well. We'll talk more about appropriate interview clothing in Chapter 28.

What NOT to Wear

Avoid bold or patterned shirts or blouses, plaid or striped suits or blouses, and anything gaudy or cheap. You want viewers to focus on your face and eyes, and not be distracted by patterns or bright colors or unnecessary bling or accessories. Ladies, focus on small tasteful earrings and possibly a discreet gold, silver or pearl necklace, but nothing too big, bold, dangly, or trendy. And absolutely show no cleavage. No tattoos, piercings, tongue rings, and the like. Read more about these items in Chapter 28.

As a general rule, avoid wearing beige, khaki, gold, orange or yellow unless you have had a professional color analysis done that shows that those colors work for you. With these colors, you run the risk of looking washed out in the photo — which is not what you want.

Personal Grooming

Men, make sure you have a nice haircut, approximately 1-2 weeks old so it has grown out a bit. Avoid facial hair if possible — it distracts the eye from seeing your face. No two-day old beard growth please!

Ladies, have your hair styled attractively and comfortably, so that it frames your face nicely, but looks easy to care for. Make up should be natural, discreet and very tasteful. Ideally, the interviewer should not even notice you are wearing makeup other than light pink lipstick. You don't want to look like a high-maintenance diva who will always be fussing with hair and makeup.

Nails should be neat and trimmed, without torn cuticles. Women should wear a light pink or natural color nail polish, French nails, or no polish. Avoid black, blue, green or multicolored nails with designs or decals. Your nails should be short enough so you can comfortably type on a keyboard.

Find a Photo Studio for a Digital Photo Shoot

Contact a local photo studio or photographer for a professional portrait sitting. Most affordable portrait studios specialize in family photography and will try to sell you packages of prints for framing and wallet photos to share. Tell them you just want a professional, corporate, résumé or digital shoot, and you want the high-resolution  digital photos instead of prints. Most studios have a professional digital package that they don't promote. It should cost somewhere between $35 and $100 maximum for one to three digital photos.

If you purchase a 3-photo package, you can select a close up shot, an upper body shot, and then another headshot in a different colored jacket or accessories for a different look.

You should select at least one photo on a white background and another headshot with a dark neutral background for flexibility in usage.

At the end of the session, you want the high resolution digital photos in a USB flash drive, or downloadable from the photographer's website, with rights to reproduce on printed materials.

If you are in college, your Career Services office may offer studio-quality photos during Career Day, so check with them to see if you can get a professional quality studio portrait for free or a low cost.

Many photo studios offer professional digital photos at affordable rates, but you should check around for the best deal. Photo studios promote heavily, so look for a deal, coupon, special promotion, or Groupon offer. You can also call the studio to negotiate a low rate in advance of booking your photo session. There will be many local photographers you can use. Here is a list of national chains that offer reasonably-priced professional digital photography:

- Picture People
- Penny's
- Target
- LifeTouch
- Olan Mills

→ TAKEAWAY — A professional photo that showcases you as bright, personable and professional is a key tool in your job search, so invest the time now to obtain your photo.

To Do List

- Take a professional portrait with several poses for use in your personal branding efforts.

- Get digital rights instead of printed portraits.

- Dress appropriately for a job interview, or like your boss will dress.

9.

Create a Professional Photo Business Card

Next, you need to create an attractive, impactful and memorable business card that will help interviewers remember you after a long job fair or a day of multiple interviews. You will use your professional business card even after you get a job and have a business card from an employer.

Vista Print is a One-stop Shop to Create Your Business Cards

You don't need to hire a graphic designer to create a fabulous business card — just go to VistaPrint for a one-stop design and print solution. Click on Business Cards to see more than 4,000 different design options.

At the bottom of the left-hand Menu box, select "Use your photos & logos" to find hundreds of great designs that will showcase your photo.

There are many places you can design and print business cards, including UPS stores and office supply stores. Most offer pricing of less than $25 for 500 to 1,000 cards.

Follow These Tips to Create Your Own Card:

- Prominently feature your photo.
- Use your professional email — never your school email.
- List your phone number with parentheses for the area code (210) 555-5555. If you use dashes instead of parentheses, it looks like a social security number, and the reader must work harder to understand what it is.
- For Title, list your job field — Marketing and Branding, or Finance and Accounting, or Social Media Management, or Video Production and Editing, or Public Relations, etc.
- Don't put a company name unless you have a consulting company of your own.
- Don't use your school name or logo.
- Select a rich, dark-colored design, rather than a more common mainly-white card – it will be more memorable.
- Print a full color back for your card.
- Select the Ultra Thick paper, or another heavy weight or distinctive paper stock — metallic, textured, pearlized for example.

- Consider upscale printing techniques, like embossing, gold foil stamping, or 3D varnish to stand out.
- Select one or two professional fonts that you want to use consistently on your professional branding materials — a bold headline font and a body copy font. Use these on your cards, on your résumé, website, and more.
- Consider rounded corners as an option to stand out.

This is your professional business card, so avoid:

- Fun, cute, or feminine graphics — no hearts, flowers, swirls, etc.
- Script and elaborate or fussy or frilly fonts
- Gaudy, dayglow or unprofessional colors
- Overly feminine or masculine look and feel
- Nicknames unless they are part of your formal professional name as listed on your résumé

Here are some impactful photo cards for both men and women to serve as examples of what can be done to create your personal branding starting with your cards.

Print 250 or 500 cards — they should cost around $25. It's an important investment in your professional image, so create your cards now and carry them with you everywhere always.

TIP — Create a Memorable Image That Links to Your Name or Other Attributes if Possible

Remember you are a brand, and like a brand, your name and image should be as memorable as possible. If your name is a color, use that color as a color signature — Mr. Brown, White, Gray, Silver, Green, etc. I met a lady who was running for an elected office, and her last name was Rojo — that's "Red" in Spanish. She wore only red — nothing else. She was distinctive and memorable and reinforced her personal branding. I worked with Mr. Green, and he always wore green, and used only green pens for writing — reinforcing his name branding. A friend whose last name is Diamond has a tasteful image of a diamond on his card; a family member whose last name is Keyes uses the image of a golden key on his card. Look for distinctive features of your name, first or last, to exploit in your self-branding.

Be Consistent with Your Image

As a Brand, so need to create a consistently positive image. Make sure you're consistent in how you present yourself, using your photo, your email signature, your name, your fonts and color scheme. Your résumé and online image today will be available to employers during online searches for the next ten years or more, so create a strong and memorable brand presence starting with your business card. If you need help, check out ways we can help you at www.BrandYouGuide.com.

➔ TAKEAWAY —— Use your marketing skills to create a powerful, professional brand image that will be consistent across all your touchpoints and over time.

- Create a memorable business card using your professional portrait.

- Print several hundred full color cards at any affordable printer — I recommend VistaPrint, but any one will do. UPS Stores also offer affordable quick-print business cards.

- Use a bold, dark or impactful color scheme to have your card stand out from all the white business cards.

- Print a bold color on the back to stand out.

- Consider other distinctive and memorable features like rounded corners, metallic ink, spot varnish or embossing to make your card stand out.

- List your profession if you don't have a specific title. Do NOT use a school email address or list your job as *"intern'*.

- Create a consistent image in all materials and over time to reinforce your personal brand.

10.

Understand Who Makes the Hiring Decision

Companies don't really hire people; people do. One particular person will recommend you for a certain job, and one person has the responsibility or clout to decide if he wants you on the team. While there may be several people on the interview panel, and you will deal with an HR (Human Resources) manager who will make you the actual offer and negotiate your employment, they are not the decision-makers. Your future boss is the decision maker.

Understand the dynamics of the job decision-making process, and reach out to the key people who will make or break your employment.

Three Different Job Targets to Reach and Influence

You have 3 different job targets when you're looking for a job:

1. The person who's going to pay you; that's your future boss.
2. The person who influences your future boss; that's his boss, other colleagues in the department, people he knows, maybe the HR manager, professional colleagues etc.
3. Your supporters or mentors who take you under their wing and help you get introduced to the other people above.

Hopefully you have found your passion and know what you want to do professionally. Next you need to figure out the people who are going to get you there.

> ⇒ TAKEAWAY — Make sure you address all 3 job targets to effectively market yourself.

11.

Find and Recruit Mentors

You need at least one mentor who is skilled at business or in your career field and will take the time and interest to guide you and help you find your dream job.

Your mentor will be someone you really connect with on a personal or professional level. It can be a more senior person in your field, a company executive, a personal family friend, a relative, or even someone you meet on another job or volunteer work.

Your mentor should help you learn how to navigate the business world or your job field and cut through the red tape by introducing you to influential people in the hiring process.

You generally have to seek out a mentor. It's okay to just flat out ask someone to become your mentor — they probably will be deeply honored or flattered that you look up to them in this manner.

You should aim for perhaps 3 or 4 active mentors to guide you in your career. You won't be in touch with them on a daily or weekly basis, but you should reach out to each of them at least once a month, by phone or by email to help you keep on track and upbeat during a difficult job search.

Remember, mentor relationships are long-term, so once you find your job, call and tell them all about it. They will appreciate knowing about your success and will likely be ready and willing to help you on your next journey in your career.

➔ TAKEAWAY — Your mentors should actively give valuable insight, build your morale, provide unique points of view, and help you connect with others in your job search. Seek out several mentors and listen to what they have to say. Their outside perspective is very valuable.

- Actively recruit between 1 and 3 mentors who will coach you in your career.

- Ask for help and guidance, and most will willingly give it.

- Touch base at least monthly to say "Hi," and update them on your progress in finding a job, or in your career path after you are employed.

12.

Line Up Your Personal and Professional References

Every employer is going to ask for references, so be prepared with a list of both personal and professional references before an employer asks for them. They will include your mentors, plus current and former employers, colleagues, vendors, customers, professors, colleagues from organizations you volunteer with. Select people who will write and say glowing things about you. Before you actively start your job search, call or talk with each of your mentors and ask if they will be willing to serve as a reference for you.

After your mentors say "Yes" to serving as a reference, make sure you have their contact information, which includes name, title, phone number, email and physical address. Create a nicely-formatted Word document with your contact information in the header or footer, and title it "References for <your name>." List each reference with contact information, and a brief one-sentence description of how you know or have worked with each person. Examples of suitable descriptions include:

- *Served on the Board of the AMA chapter together from 2014-2016*
- *Direct supervisor at XYZ Corporation; can attest to my team work skills and attention to detail*
- *Ad agency account executive; worked together on the XYZ account*
- *Youth Ministry Pastor of XYZ church; worked together to host the summer Vacation Bible Camp in 2015*
- *Professor of Marketing for 3 courses from 2015-2016; can speak to my work ethic and dedication to my passion for marketing*
- *Customer from 2010 - 2013; provided accounting services to his family-run landscaping business*
- *Business executive, longtime family friend; familiar with personal background and values*

Take several copies of this list of references to your job interview. If the company seems interested, leave one copy with the HR director. Keep one handy to use in filling out the Job Application, which they will probably ask you to complete, even though they have your detailed résumé.

Save the file in both Word and PDF format, so you can forward it to your HR contact with a follow-up email to thank them for your interview.

TIP — Shortcut to Filling Out the Job Application Form
Even through you may have already filled out an online application, HR will undoubtedly ask you to fill out a long and tedious hard copy application form during an in-person interview. What they really need is your signature giving them the legal right to contact former employers for references and to perform credit and criminal background searches.

Shortcut the application by filling out just the contact information, Social Security number (make sure you have it memorized), anything that's NOT on your résumé or list of references, and signing and dating the application. Write in pen *"See attached résumé"* on all sections covered by your résumé. Then attach your résumé and list of references to the application with a paperclip (which you will bring in your briefcase) and hand it in to HR. It will look much better than trying to hand-write lots of information into too-tiny spaces, and your application will be clean and neat. Five minutes and you're done!

Let Each Reference Know to Expect a Call — And Coach Them on a Suggested Response

After sharing the list of references with a prospective employer, call each listed reference and let them know that they may receive a call asking for a reference. Tell them something like, *"I just applied for a job at XYZ corporation working in social media marketing for their automobile insurance division, and I listed you as a reference. Hopefully, you will get a phone call. If you do hear from them, I'd really appreciate it if you mentioned what a good job we did together on the Jones account last year and how we grew sales by 27%."*

You don't want them to just say, *"Yeah, she worked for me — I don't remember when."* You can benefit from reminding them of dates, stats accomplishments, and specifics that they can mention so their talking points will be fresh on their minds.

Lastly, ask them to give you a quick call if they DO get contacted by HR to let you know specific questions they asked, if they appeared to have any concerns or interest, and what your reference said about you. It will help you gauge how likely you are to get an offer.

TIP — Understand What Former Employers May and May Not Say About You

In today's litigious society, employers are hesitant to say too much or too little about you for fear of being sued. Each state has a different law about what can and cannot be disclosed in response to a request for employment verification, from almost nothing to a great deal of information — some of which you may not want revealed. If a prospective employer calls an HR department, the information they will receive is limited. The most they might receive is confirmation of:

- Whether or not you were ever employed by the company
- Your title or position
- Your dates of employment
- Your compensation level — confirmation of what you stated you earned
- Whether or not you are eligible to be rehired — it's the legal way to find out if you were fired or left in bad standing

---

→ TAKEAWAY — Your list of references is very important because it gets beyond the barrier of the HR department to put a prospective employer in touch with someone who will give you a rave review.

To Do List

- Make a list of professional and personal references and have on hand at or after an interview.

- Include name, current contact information, and info on how you worked together in the past.

- Call or email to get permission to use each as a reference before finalizing the list.

- Call each reference when you expect a company to check your references to coach them on dates and key projects and achievements.

13.

Get an Internship —
The #1 Way to Land Your Job

 The single best way to get a job is to have an internship in your desired field. It's even better if you have 2 or 3! So don't wait until the summer before your senior year of college to apply for internships. The more relevant work experience you have on your résumé, the easier it's going to be to get a great professional job.

Paid vs Unpaid?

Of course you and every student want an internship with a prestigious company that pays you a huge amount of money. If you can find an internship that pays you $10 or $15 an hour, take it. There are few paid internships, and they are highly sought after. Hundreds or even thousands of students may be competing for that one great paid internship with a premier company. If you can get selected, you're a job-hunting superhero.

The sad truth is that most internships are not paid. But what matters to a potential employer is the experience and job skills you gained during the internship. Many unpaid internships with smaller companies provide you with more hands-on experience and exposure than structured internships with big companies.

And, it is so infinitely easier to land an unpaid internship than a paid one.

I've had probably 30 or 40 interns over the years, and I have never paid any of them, for good reasons.

First and foremost, in recent years I have generally worked for small start-up or entrepreneurial companies that don't have many resources. The money that I might pay to an intern could be invested somewhere else for a greater return.

Just as importantly, when I hire you as an intern, I'm going to invest a significant amount of my very valuable time training and mentoring you. It is a big investment of time and effort on my part.

I do consulting for national companies, and I bill at $100 an hour. If I sit down and spend 3 hours of my time talking to you, that's $300 that I've invested in you. So I can't afford to pay you a salary on top of that investment.

Big Companies Have Different Issues

Large, well-structured companies have strict HR and management policies, and one of these concerns is headcount. Each department must receive approval for the number of people who work there — it's called headcount. Headcount is budgeted in the annual operating budget, reported monthly, and measured by HR. Revenues, productivity and profitability are often benchmarked per employee — Sales per Employee is a common performance metric.

The Human Resource department and senior leadership must approve every single position in every single department. They have to set you up as an employee, complete an onboarding program, process a huge amount of paperwork, sign you up for payroll and automatic payroll deposit, set up income tax withholding, and more. If it's a paid  internship, and they have to report the increased headcount, they're not going to do it. It's just too much work.

So getting a paid internship may not be realistic unless you are an academic superstar. If you can get one, wonderful; but if you can't, take an unpaid internship, especially early in school, shooting for a prestigious paid internship your senior year when you have more experience on your résumé.

But there may be ways to get some compensation from an internship. Ask for a stipend to cover out-of-pocket costs. Ask *"Can you give me $100 a week educational stipend to pay for my mileage, parking, tolls and mobile phone?"* You might be able to get that because companies will process that as an expense report and not payroll — a much easier process.

Create Your Own Internship

While some unpaid internships may be posted on your college job board, most companies simply don't bother to create an internship posting or ad. Small companies don't have the time or contacts to post unpaid internships with different schools.

So identify the company you want to work for, network with the person you want to work for, and say, *"I want to work for you and your company. Would you let me work as an intern? I'll work for free for the next three months."* Voila — you have just created your own internship!

5 Ways to Maximize the Return on Your Internship Investment

When you work as an intern, especially an unpaid intern, you are making an investment in the company. You are investing your time, talents, and wages that you would have earned bagging groceries or washing cars. Plus, if you take a supervised internship for credit through your university, you may have to pay thousands of dollars of tuition for the right to work for free! So you need to earn a good return on that investment. Here are 5 ways to monetize any internship, paid or unpaid:

1. List the Internship as a Job on Your Résumé

With a smaller company, you may be able to negotiate a more attractive title instead of "Intern." Ask for a title — or make up one and suggest it. Think of non-traditional titles that give you a position outside of the corporate hierarchy — Social Media Scheduler, Marketing Assistant, Sales Support Technician, Media Analyst, Lab Assistant, Research Apprentice, Event Planning Aide, Auxiliary Producer, etc. Avoid corporate titles that have a generally accepted meaning: Director, Manager, Executive, etc. Use undefined titles like Assistant, Aide, Apprentice, Technician, Support, etc. And when you interview for a job, don't say it was an internship, or whether or not it was paid. It was a job. Period.

2. Ask for a Business Card

A business card is really cheap for a company to print — most will print 250 cards for under $20 from a preferred vendor who has the company template already set up. That is a small investment for the company to make, but worth a great deal in your networking and career development. Showing a real business card for a real company pegs you as a peer when meeting other professionals, and allows you to interact with them as a professional and not as a college student or job applicant. So ask for one.

3. Create a Professional Hard Copy Portfolio

Collect samples of everything you do during your internship, plus projects that you legitimately worked on and supported, even if you were not solely responsible for the project execution. Then create a powerful hard copy portfolio to showcase your work. Add "show and tell" materials from prior jobs, school projects or class work, volunteer work, even made-up work to demonstrate your skills.

Buy a nice presentation portfolio with oversized plastic sleeves to insert your samples. In the back, add your résumé, your references, copies of recommendation letters, copies of awards, prizes, certificates, scholarship award letters, college transcripts, newspaper and magazine clippings of a professional nature, and more. Arrange these nicely and artistically so they tell a story. An interviewer may ask, "Tell me about yourself," and you can whip out your portfolio and say, "Let me show you what I am passionate about." Then walk him through the portfolio like you are telling a story. Something magical happens during this process — you become excited and dynamic and passionate when you explain these interesting projects you have worked on, and that enthusiasm is contagious — they will think you are wonderful.

4. **Create an Online Portfolio**

    Scan, photograph, and digitize all the samples and materials that go into your hard copy portfolio, and use these to create a powerful online portfolio that you can easily share with a prospective employer through an email link or hyperlink on your résumé and LinkedIn page. For free online resources, check out Pathbrite and Issuu. LinkedIn recommends these five sites for online portfolios for creatives — Carbonmade, DROPR, Cargo Collective, Behance.net, and Coroflot. LinkedIn even allows you to post attachments and photos in your profile and create shareable files in their SlideShare program. Your school or university may also offer a free online portfolio – ask Career Services.

5. **Get Glowing Letters of Recommendation**

    At the end of your internship, ask for a letter of recommendation from your boss, from his boss, from the president of the company, from vendors, from customers, from anyone you have dealt with in a positive manner. Ask for a hard copy of the letter if possible, and then scan it and make copies. Never give away the original — keep it in your portfolio forever!

    Many people will say *"I don't have the time to write a letter. Write a draft of what you want me to say and let me look at it."* So incredible as it may seem, you get to write your own recommendation letters! Put your modesty away and write rave reviews about yourself that are honest and realistic. Think *"If I were in her shoes, how would she look at me? What would she say about me?"* and then you write that letter. Discuss accomplishments, projects done, results achieved. Mention positive attributes and skills honed in the field that you want highlighted. The last line should always offer a phone number and email address for more information.

    If you write a good and objective letter, the majority of the time, they will look at it, sign it and send it back.

Keep a packet of photocopies of letters of recommendation, preferably in color and stapled together, which you can give to the interviewer after he has looked at the originals. These letters of recommendation are very, very valuable. Never ever give your original signed letters of recommendation away. You scan each one, you photocopy them, then you put them in your hard copy portfolio. I have copies of letters of recommendation from my bosses from thirty years ago and they're still in my portfolio, on letterhead, embossed and signed, available for inspection.

What if You're Not in School Right Now?

If you are in any formal program of study, you can apply for an internship, paid or unpaid. Many universities offer structured internship programs, or you can just apply on your own for the experience, even if you are not currently taking a class.

If you are not enrolled in any formal degree program, or have already graduated, it is more difficult, because you may not qualify for the more common unpaid internships, due to Department of Labor regulations.

To gain the desired work experience, you have 2 options:

- **Apply to a college or university** – your acceptance should satisfy the Fair Labor Practices concerns. Companies have legal limitations concerning unpaid internships, and if you're not currently in school, it would be a risk for them to have you work for less than minimum wage.
- **Volunteer for a non-profit organization in the field you want to work in**. There are thousands of non-profits that desperately need help in doing just about everything as they are all chronically understaffed and underfunded. Tell them you want to work in the specific department or functional area of your choice to gain experience, and they will generally accommodate your request. They may even offer you a business card from the organization and an attractive title — if not, ask for it. There are many different types of non-profits that will provide you valuable experience, including churches, homeless shelters, food banks, veterans' organizations, children's groups  like Boy Scouts and Girl Scouts, medical services charities and foundations, programs for the aged, arts programs, cultural groups, trade associations, and so many more. One important benefit you might receive is to meet influential community leaders who serve on the board or make donations to the group. List this volunteer work as a job on your résumé or as a client for your consulting firm.

➔ TAKEAWAY — Any internship should provide valuable job experience which will allow you to get a more prestigious internship in the future, and help you land a great job after college. Whether it's a paid or unpaid internship, focus on the skills and experiences you have gained, and monetize the internship to help you in your job search.

- Actively seek out an internship early in your college career, and each summer if possible.

- Consider an unpaid internship if you don't find a great paid internship.

- Seek out internships with both big prestigious companies and small firms – that may offer the best experience and exposure.

- If the company you want to work for doesn't currently have an internship available, create one by volunteering to work for them at no charge for 3 months.

- Maximize the ROI of your internship investment of time and efforts whenever possible.

- Volunteer for a non-profit organization in the role you are seeking in order to gain needed experience and credentials.

14.

Create Your Powerful Résumé

One of the most powerful tools in your job-hunting toolbox is a strong and effective résumé. It will make or break your job search, so you must craft a strong, persuasive and enticing one. You want a résumé that HR will like, your future boss will be intrigued with, and the search engines and web crawlers will find and showcase.

It must be perfect in grammar and spelling, be pleasing to the reader's eye, and formatted to draw the reader's attention quickly to the important information.

It's not just me. 61% of recruiters and 43 % of hiring managers will discard your résumé because of a single typo or misspelling.

According to *BeHiring.com,* the average recruiter conducting a preliminary screening will spend just six seconds reviewing your résumé, so it's important that the four key items he is looking for jump out immediately:

- Job titles
- Name of employers
- Start and end dates of employment
- Education

Let's start with the hard copy résumé first — the one you will present to a potential employer at a face-to-face meeting.

Eight Sections to a Great Résumé

A great résumé has 8 sections, presented in a specific order. Make sure you understand the purpose and formatting for each one. Here is how these should be organized from top to bottom.

What to include in a resume?

- ☑ objective
- ☑ education & qualifications
- ☑ work experience & accomplishment
- ☑ skills & personal strengths
- ☑ training experience
- ☑ languages
- ☑ hobbies & interests
- ☑ social activities

1. **Name and Contact Information**

   Use your professional name at the top of the résumé, in bold caps or otherwise highlighted so it jumps off the page and is easy to see. Underneath that, list your contact information: your professional

   email address, your phone number formatted (123) 456-7890 with parentheses instead of dashes or dots. You can add a Skype address, a LinkedIn address, or the address of your online portfolio. Embed the link in your document if you will distribute it online or submit it to an online site.

   Have two versions of your résumé, one with your mailing address and one without. An out-of-town address may cause a potential employer to discard your résumé to avoid relocation expense. So if you are applying for an out-of-town position, use the résumé without an address.

2. **Career Objective**

   You need to tell a prospective employer exactly what kind of a job you are looking for, and in what field. If you don't have a stated objective, the employer may not know what you want to do and will go on to the next résumé.

   I had a great student with a lot of unrelated work experience, and her résumé didn't have a job objective. She had worked as a nanny for five years, while putting herself through college to earn a business degree in marketing. So the logical question was *"Are you applying for a job as a nanny?"* Of course not, she wanted a job in marketing. Without clearly stating that goal, a prospective employer would not make sense of her résumé. So write a very specific job objective, such as:

   - *Entry-level position in brand management for a leading CPG company*
   - *Senior Account Executive position in a B2C digital marketing agency*
   - *Staff Accountant, with focus on accounts receivable and collections*
   - *Executive Director for a non-profit organization serving the local community*
   - *Production Supervisor for a thermoform plastic manufacturer*

   Then you will enhance that objective by stating some of your relevant skills that make you a perfect match for the job (this is where those unpaid internships pay off in spades!) Therefore, the full job description might read:

Entry-level position in brand management for a leading CPG company, utilizing my experience in qualitative and quantitative marketing research, social media content creation, and consumer event management, supported by an MBA with a concentration in consumer marketing.

You will have one basic résumé with your most desired career objective which you will place on LinkedIn. But you will need to customize each résumé you send out to the posted job and company. This section should clearly state how your career objective exactly matches the job description by mirroring the wording of the job posting.

That's right, I said "mirror." By this I mean use the exact same words and phrases as in the job posting. This is important because many of the jobs you will be applying for are listed online, and recruiters and headhunters use key word searches to find prospective candidates. By mirroring the wording of the job posting and requirements, your résumé will match the search criteria, and the computer should flag your résumé as a good match.

3. **Summary of Skills, Qualifications, or Overview**

This is a brief summary of relevant skills you offer, and lists why the company should hire you. Often, employers won't read past this section, so you need to give them compelling reasons they should hire you.

If you are sending a generic résumé without a specific job description, create a brief summary of skills in a bulleted format of credentials and specific skills or talents that showcase quantifiable information. Avoid the fluff. *"Good team player"* and *"hardworking and motivated"* are throwaway words in this section.

If you are personalizing the résumé to a specific job description, make a comparison between the job requirements on the posting, and show how you meet or exceed them. Use the exact language of the job posting to highlight your relevant qualifications.

Job Requirements	My Credentials
Min. B. A. degree	B.A. in Business Administration from Texas A&M 2015
3 years experience	5+ years related work experience in Sales, Customer Service, Marketing
Excellent computer skills	Proficient in Microsoft Office Suite – Word, PowerPoint, Excel, Publisher, Access; Photoshop; Illustrator; Quark Express; WordPress; QuickBooks

Personalize this list for each job you apply for to ensure the skills match the list of job requirements. Be concise, and consider arranging the list in columns like this example to save space.

4. **Education**

Depending upon the amount of your professional experience, the 4th section of your résumé will either be Education or Professional Experience. If you have limited relevant work experience but a college degree, or if you are getting ready to graduate, start with Education. If you have valuable work experience in your field, or haven't finished college, start with Experience.

This list should be in reverse chronological order, with most recent education first, and oldest education last. Unless you had great accomplishments in high school that did not continue into college (National Merit Scholar or state football champion, for example), start with college and leave high school off your résumé.

You should include this information for each school:

- The degree, major and minor, year awarded — for example *B.A. in Business Administration, Major in Marketing, Minor in French, 2014.* If you're currently in college right now, list your expected graduation date — *Expected graduation May 2017*
- The name of the university, city and state — *Middlebury College, Middlebury VT*
- Special awards and recognition — *Cum Laude, class valedictorian, Dean's List 6 semesters, member of Phi Beta Kappa Honor Society, etc.*
- Academic rank or GPA — *GPA 3.8/4.0, ranked 17th in class of 425, top 10% of class, etc.* If your GPA is below 3.0, you might want to list your GPA during the last 2 years, or your GPA in your major. If your academic performance was poor, leave your GPA out altogether.
- Activities — Athletics (list varsity sports and special achievement), school organizations and clubs, fraternities, elected positions, volunteer positions or extracurricular activities, service learning, foreign studies, etc. This section about your school years should grab people's attention that will cause them to want to meet you.
- Scholarships — Mention scholarships you have received and the sponsoring organization.

- Other information — If you worked to support yourself, add *"100% self-supporting"* (or whatever percentage is accurate) or *"financed 100% of education by working 40 hours a week."*

5. **Professional Experience**

Your Professional Experience also should be listed in reverse chronological order, oldest at the bottom, most recent at the top. Organize your listing either by company name first, or by title, depending upon which is more impressive. If you worked for a prestigious company like IBM or Coca-Cola, list the company first. If you worked for an unknown company, you may want to list your title first, then the company name, and a one or two-word description so the recruiter knows it was a CPA firm, law office, construction company, IT service company, etc. Whichever format you choose, be consistent throughout the document. Add the city and state (use the 2-letter state abbreviation), and the years of employment on the first line if possible. Try to format the document so the years end up flush right, easy to see during a quick scan of the résumé. This line of the résumé should probably be bold or underlined or both to easily stand out.

On the next line, add a brief one-sentence description of key job responsibilities or functions, and brief information about the company or division if needed for clarity. Avoid company jargon or company-specific terms.

Then list in bullet form your key quantifiable accomplishments — not activities or responsibilities — starting with action verbs in the past tense for prior jobs, and in present tense for your current job. If possible, add a time frame or period. Check out these examples:

- *Spearheaded 12% growth through new CRM system in FY 2014*
- *Increased customer count by 500 new members (+8%) in a 4-month period*
- *Reduced quality control rejects by 17% through implementation of a vendor pre-certification program over 2 years*
- *Generated $500,000 of direct sales of computer peripherals in first year*
- *Beat sales quota by 37% in 2016*
- *Received President's Award as top 5% of national sales force in 2012*
- *Created and posted 87 new social media and blog posts to support line expansion*

Present information in this section is consistently and attractively, with the job title, employers' names and dates of employment easy to find in a quick scan. These are the 3 items any recruiter will look for first, so they need to pop out quickly during an initial scan.

6. **Other Employment**

Here's where you list those years as a nanny, working for the Geek Squad, stocking grocery shelves, selling Mary Kay, or brewing coffee at Starbucks. It is your opportunity to showcase longevity of employment, training experiences and certifications, performance excellence if possible (being McDonald's employee of the month for 4 months does matter!), and varied experiences that might be of interest. I once interviewed and hired a man who worked with a large comic book company because the company caught my eye. I recently had a student who had been a professional jockey — that caused me to stop and take notice of him and his dedication to a profession, even if unrelated to his current field. Use this section to stand out from the crowd and say something powerful about your work ethic and dedication. Only list jobs with longevity of employment, relevant or transferrable skills, or rewards and recognition for achievement.

7. **Skills and Expertise**

Computer Skills — List your computer skills here — these are critical in today's market. Basic knowledge of the Microsoft Office suite is essential, but not everyone is skilled at Publisher or WordPress, so highlight these if you know them. Mastery of the Adobe Creative Suite is very impressive — Photoshop, Illustrator, InDesign are important, as well as any video editing and web development software if you want to work in business, marketing or creative fields. Also list any specialty software expertise you have — CAD/CAM, GIS, banking/finance software, QuickBooks, PMP or Project Management software, etc. Don't mention overly basic programs like Google, Facebook, LinkedIn, etc.

Foreign Languages — List languages other than English, and indicate your mastery level — *fluent, intermediate, beginning.*

Certifications and Licenses — List any certifications that are relevant to your business, such as *PMP (Project Management), CPA, Insurance and Financial Services certifications, Cordon Bleu, etc.*

8. **Additional Information**

Awards — If you have awards or prizes other than those listed under Education, list these here.

Professional Associations — List memberships in your professional associations, including Board positions or volunteer roles. Virtually every industry has one or more professional or trade associations, and you should join, participate and volunteer. We'll talk more about that when we discuss networking.

Military Service — Provide branch, rank, job assignment, specialized training, key assignments, awards and recognition, etc.

Non-job Related Activities — List volunteer work, boards you sit on, leadership positions you have held, and prestigious memberships (skip *Who's Who* — everyone gets that.) List organizations that tell the recruiter good things about you — belonging to Mensa (*says you are very smart*), volunteering for Big Brothers & Big Sisters (*says that you care),* being a Guardian ad Litem (*you are civic minded*), volunteering for Habitat for Humanity (*you are actively engaged in improving your community*), etc.

Citizenship and Work Status — If you are a US citizen, state it. If you are a foreign national, indicate your immigration status, *"I am a Saudi citizen in the United States on a student visa, able to participate in unpaid internships,"* or something like that, because otherwise your work status will be a barrier to consideration.

Willingness to Relocate or Travel — If you are willing to relocate for the job, say so. If you are not able or willing to move, it's your choice to state it or not. You might leave it out, and then if they really want you, you might be able to negotiate a remote position — work from your home or a satellite office. If you are willing and able to travel for work, list it here.

Unusual Skills or Hobbies — List sports or unusual activities you participate in like marathons or Iron Man competitions, golf, tennis, racquetball, fly fishing – the possibilities are endless. Men love talking about sports, so add sports information and you may make a great impression if your interviewer is a fan or participant in the same sport. Highlight expertise in the arts — music, art, dance, etc. Mention extensive international travel — *"Exchange student in Norway for 8 months"* or *"toured with Up With People to China and the Far East."* Showcase activities that portray you as an interesting, stimulating, curious and engaged person — the kind of person the interviewer would like to have as a friend or colleague.

Examples of Good Résumés

Let's see what some effective résumé formatting styles look like. See more full-sized examples at the end of this chapter, and on the BrandYouGuide.com website.

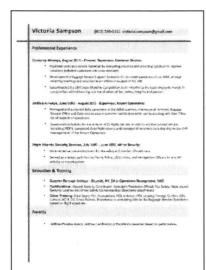

Formatting Your Résumé

Think of your résumé like an advertising brochure or flier — it needs to be attractive, easy to read, visually interesting, and able to deliver your sales pitch efficiently before your "customer" moves on to the next brochure.

Your résumé should be attractively formatted, with a combination of bold texts, capitals, underlining and italics to guide the reader easily and quickly from section to section, highlighting the key information. Use white space to guide the reader and provide a visually soothing reading experience. If it's jumbled together and too busy, it will be harder to read and comprehend, and the reader will likely lose focus and interest.

It is preferable to use a serif font like Times New Roman or Bookman. A serif font is one with the little squiggles at the top and bottom of the letter. It is the font used by newspapers, because it is easier on the eye than a non-serif font.

Use a 10, 11, or 12 font size; anything smaller will be too hard to read. Anything larger will look childish.

Unless you have many years of experience and many jobs, limit your résumé to one page.

Proofread your résumé and have others do the same. You can't have one single error, typo, incorrect word usage, or poor grammar. Not one. Even one error will cause the reader to immediately quit reading and move on to the next candidate.

Preparing Your Résumé for Online Submission

When you are sending your résumé by email, make sure you do not label your attachment just *"résumé."* You can't imagine the number of résumés I receive without the candidate's name in the title of the file. If your résumé is titled *"résumé,"* I will save it in my computer folder of submitted résumés and it will overwrite the last résumé from someone else that was titled *"résumé."* Then the next file labeled just *"résumé"* will overwrite your file. Just as important, I will never be able to find your file if it's not labeled correctly.

Title your file with your first and last name, your desired job, and then "résumé." You can add year if you wish. The goal is to have it easily identifiable by the recipient if she wants to look it up in her files. It can look like any of these examples:

- DianeHuthRésumé-2016-VP Marketing
- DianeHuth-Résumé-VP-Marketing
- Diane_Huth_Résumé _2016_VPMarketing
- Diane-Huth-Résumé -VPMktg-2016

No matter which naming format you choose, it will be crystal clear that the file is a résumé, whose résumé it is, what the desired position is, and when the file was submitted.

The same thing is true for the subject line of your email — make sure it is clear and includes your professional name along with the word "*résumé*" so it can be easily found in an email search.

Unless your job posting instructions say differently, submit your résumé in both Word and PDF format. Your Word résumé can be scanned by all scanning programs, while many can't read a PDF. On the other hand, a PDF can be opened on any device, and saved to your Book folder on a phone or tablet for sharing and forwarding. Also, with a PDF, you can be confident that there won't be any file reading problem when received by email.

Make sure your résumé is loaded with the right key words which match the job requirements which the search spiders will be looking for. Just as in social media, you need to SEO your résumé to ensure Search Engine Optimization. Mention key words early in the document, especially in the Objective and Overview sections. Use multiple words to describe the same item to maximize search results — for example, "social media" "digital media," "online media" might all describe the same activities and be used interchangeably and thus may be picked up separately by the search engines. And mirror the job posting language to insert the identical key words in your résumé.

TIP — Consider "Ghostwriting" Keywords

One debated technique suggested by a friend Alan Hanefeld is to "ghostwrite" keywords on the bottom or even side of your résumé. In essence, you create a text block of key words, and then set the color to white. The human eye won't see them, but the search spiders will find them and match them against the job specifications.

Don't Put Your Photo on Your Résumé

HR is mandated to eliminate potential discrimination based on race and ethnicity and appearance for government compliance reasons. They want an objective résumé that eliminates bias or discrimination, so about half of all recruiters will reject a résumé with a photo. However, you want them to like you and remember you over all other candidates. So unless your appearance would be detrimental to the selection process, my suggestion is to mail a résumé without a photo, but paper clip your business card (with your photo on it of course) to the résumé you are hand-delivering or mailing, so the interviewer will remember you. It's the same thing when you are applying for a job by cold calling the company — whenever possible, mail a hardcopy of your résumé or even better your "Broadcast Letter" (more about this in the next chapter), with your business card clipped to it to stand out in the selection process.

Avoid Taboo Topics

- **Do not mention or include politics or political party affiliation**, unless it is your paid job. Half of the people you interview with will be from the other party, and they may think poorly of you for "bad judgement" for supporting a candidate or party they dislike.
- **Do not mention your religion if possible**. If your volunteer work of note includes work at your religious institution, just mention something like: *Lay Minister, church organist, head of church youth group, church choir member*. If the interviewer asks about it, of course feel free to discuss your religious affiliation at that time.
- **Don't mention anything negative**. Do not say or write anything negative about any former employer or colleague, even if you left the employment against your will or quit over a bad situation. Prospective employers may see you as being petty and vindictive.

Keep it Short!

Unless you have many years of experience and more than 3 or 4 professional jobs, keep your résumé to 1 page. For older professionals with a large number of jobs, I suggest you have 2 résumés — a 1-page summary résumé that just shows highlights of companies, titles and dates, and a full 2-page résumé with all the accomplishments detailed. Never allow your résumé to run more than 2 pages.

If you are an academic, with multiple advanced degrees and published papers, applying for a job teaching at a university or research laboratory, you will probably want to use a CV — Curriculum Vitae — which contains all the gory details in many pages. Google to find the right formatting for a CV.

Seek Out Expert Opinion About Your Résumé

Once you think your résumé is perfect, ask objective third parties for their opinion, help and suggestions. Here are great tools and resources to fine tune your résumé:

- Show it to friends, teachers, counselors, mentors, etc. They know you well and may think of strengths you overlooked. And they can definitely help you proofread for typos and grammar!
- Go to Job Services at your school. You probably can get help from your school mentoring program, or even your Alumni Office for no charge.
- Go to your favorite job-seeking website — Monster, Indeed, Ladders, etc. — and purchase résumé writing help. Expect to pay around $100 to fine tune and format your résumé.
- Go to an independent résumé writing service. There are dozens more that you can find by a simple Google search. Again, expect to pay between $100 and $200.
- I am available to help write or revise your résumé and format it beautifully at www.BrandYouGuide.com.

➔ TAKEAWAY — Your résumé is your most critical tool in finding a job. Invest your time and expertise in creating a powerful résumé and invest your money if needed to make sure it represents you in the most professional and persuasive way possible. Then personalize it for every single job application, inserting key words to be found by computer search programs that conduct the preliminary screening and selection before a human sees the résumé.

- Create a powerful and persuasive résumé.

- Get professional help to write and format your résumé and job hunting materials.

- Understand the purpose and content of each of the 8 sections of a résumé.

- Personalize each résumé to the specific job being applied for by mirroring the key words of the job descriptions and qualifications.

Make sure your résumé is perfect – not a single typo or bad grammar.

Ryan Christopher Martin
10255 Red Stone– San Antonio, TX 78227
Tel: (210) 424-6703 – Email: Ryan.Martin3@gmail.com

OVERVIEW
Freshman attending UNC, majoring in Mechanical Engineering. High School Honors Graduate. Member of American Mensa, with demonstrated ability to learn new skills quickly and efficiently. Motivated to gain wide ranging experience and learn business and technical skills. Seeking part time employment while attending college in an area that provides learning experience and skills development, while making valuable contribution to my employer.

UNC – FRESHMAN MECHANICAL ENGINEERING MAJOR
- Estimated Graduation 2017
- 9 Credit Hours from Dual Credit Classes and AP Tests

CHURCHILL HIGH SCHOOL
- Graduated Cum Laude June 2014
- 3.7 GPA, 94 Average
- SAT score 1170 (Verbal and Math), 1700 total
- High school Chess Club officer 2005-2008

EMPLOYMENT:
- **Hometown Pizza Company – Redemption and Customer Service (January-May 2007)**
  - **Responsibilities:** Direct sales to children and parents, Cashier, stocked over 200 merchandise items daily, customer service and problem resolution
  - **Awards and Recognition:**
    - #1 ranked sales rep during 4 consecutive months
    - Consistently sold $800 - $1000 on weekends – double all other sales employees
    - Received "Joker" award for positive attitude and enthusiasm

VOLUNTEER AND HOBBY:
- Assisted Counseling Office personnel to develop and maintain database of student award records
- Volunteered at Texas Service and Hearing Dog Association fundraiser programs
- Sony Online Electronics Guide Program - Volunteer Guide - online customer service (Summer 2006)
- Volunteer at Mensa Annual Gathering programs 2007 and 2008
- Fitness and exercise, weight lifting

TRAVEL
- **International**: Japan, Thailand

OTHER:
- US citizen
- Excellent computer skills: Word, PowerPoint, Excel,
- Member of American Mensa – attended 2007 and 2008 Annual Gatherings
- References available upon request

Jessica Kent

148 Cargo Street • San Antonio, TX 78220
(210) 771-6644 • Jessica.Kent@yahoo.com

Career Objective

I am seeking a challenging entry level position in marketing and social media, which will build upon my work experience and educational background. I am hardworking, inquisitive, and diligent, with excellent writing skills. I seek to continue to gain experience and expertise in a wide range of marketing functions, and to be able to contribute to my employer's business success.

Education

Bachelor of Business Administration in Marketing - Texas A&M University, San Antonio   May 2017
- GPA 3.2 / 4.0, National Society of Leadership and Success Member

Associates of Arts, St. Philip's College - San Antonio TX   2013 - 2015
- Associate of Arts in Economics - December 2015
- Associate of Arts in Liberal Arts - May 2015
- GPA 3.29 / 4.0
- Dean's List, 100% self supporting

Professional Experience

Biovideo LLC, San Antonio, TX - Social Media Manger   February 2015 - Present
Innovative maternity videography market leader, serving new parents in Texas and Mexico
- Responsible for maintenance of all company social media sites, including creation of content, managing posting schedule, online contests and affiliate accounts
- Experience with Facebook, Twitter, Pinterest, Instagram, LinkedIn, Google+
- Content creation for different media properties
- Overall exposure to various aspects of marketing, research, sales support, and more

Walt Disney Company - Orlando FL   Merchandising Intern   August 2014 - January 2015
Participated in 6-month collegiate internship and training program at Disney World in Orlando FL. Worked in a range of merchandising positions throughout the park. Participated in company orientation and training programs, gaining insight from corporate leaders and department managers in a wide range of functional areas. Excellent overview of how a world-class entertainment property maintains global leadership position through continued excellence in all areas of operation.

American Red Cross, San Antonio TX   Office Intern   June 2013 – August 2013
Internship at Red Cross regional office, providing administrative support to the office manager. Conducted mass mailings, compiled and analyzed data, internal communication. Excellent overview of how a premier non-profit operates.

Six Flags Fiesta Texas, San Antonio TX   Retail Hostess and Merchandiser   May 2009 – July 2013
Gained valuable experience in hospitality retailing and merchandising, entertainment industry

Computer Skills

Microsoft Office Word Certified: Access, PowerPoint, and Outlook; Excel, PhotoShop

Honors and Activities
- Member, Randolph Brooks Federal Credit Union Youth Advisory Council, 2010-2012
- Dean's List 5 semesters
- Recipient of 7 academic scholarships

AMANDA PETERSON

11 Austin Highway, San Antonio TX
Amanda.T.Peterson@gmail.com
(210) 863 - 7706

Summary of Qualifications

- Strong background successfully managing organizations to achieve business goals
- Persistent and driven; acquired BBA while maintaining a fulltime job
- Creative and detail-oriented; strong eye for aesthetics
- Exceptional listener and communicator, both verbally and in writing
- Proficient in a variety of software applications, including Microsoft Office suite
- Reliable and trustworthy, maintaining flexibility in multiple environments

Professional Experience

Air Force Youth Services, Whiteman AFB, MO - Youth Services Coordinator
May 2011 – Apr. 2014
Planned, coordinated and conducted activities for program participants based on observed needs. Implemented activities and special events that met the physical, social, emotional and cognitive needs of children and youth. Developed and executed 7 weekly clubs and over 10 annual events, reaching over 10,000 members of the military community.

Buzzy Bees Daycare, San Antonio, TX - Assistant Director - Jan. 2012 – Mar. 2014
Managed 20 employees and oversaw day-to-day business operations. Responsible for obtaining new-hires and prospective families for the childcare facility. Organized medical and personnel records of employees and 60+ children.

Other Work Experience

The Jones Household, San Antonio, TX - Caretaker, April 2014 – present
Manage the safety and well-being of two children, one with a serious medical condition. Organize daily routine and activities, while balancing medications and environmental adjustments as needed.

Education

University of the Incarnate Word, San Antonio, TX
Currently obtaining a B.B.A. in Marketing, graduating Spring 2018
Business GPA: 3.43
Marketing GPA: 3.65

Personal

Relocating to San Jose CA upon graduation to join my husband on assignment with the Air Force
References available upon request

Alexander Taylor Hunt

7600 Callaghan Road #403, San Antonio TX 78239
Tel: (210) 434-0191 – Email: AlexanderTHunt@gmail.com

OVERVIEW

Graduating senior majoring in Management with team leadership experience, professional presentation skills, and a strong consulting internship background seeking to fulfill long term goal of working at leading consulting or technology firm.

EMPLOYMENT

- **ACCENTURE – Intern – San Antonio, TX**   May 2017– Present
  - Provide comprehensive support to team working on $5 B business development goal
  - Recognized throughout the team as the go-to person for high quality research
  - Assist in authoring proposals for new contracts
  - Develop and present briefs to internal and external staff
  - Consistently met and exceeded deadlines in high pressure situations to support staff

- **GEEKSQUAD AT BESTBUY - Counter Intelligence Agent – San Antonio, TX**   May 2014 – April 2017
  - Delivered computer setup, troubleshooting, and repair services
  - Used as go-to sales support by management for difficult sales
  - Worked as key team member to provide above-and-beyond customer service, reduced turnaround time on units to the best in the district, and exceed service sales goals

- **SYSCO FOODS – Intern – Portland, OR**   May 2010 – August 2010
  - Supported senior project engineer in large, heavily automated factory
  - Created tutorials and best practices for engineering department on managing OS shell and backups
  - Documented and labeled entire 5 story factory LAN infrastructure, creating maps and spreadsheets for future reference

- **ANDREWS CONSULTING ENGINEERS – Intern - San Antonio, TX**   May 2009 – August 2009
  - Provided assistance for leading global engineering firm specializing in civil engineering and risk analysis
  - Creation of comprehensive chemical database in Excel, emphasizing reactive properties
  - Performed 2D and 3D CAD modeling, generating 3D models from walkthrough pictures

EDUCATION

- **UTSA – Bachelor of Business Administration in Management**   May 2017
  - 3.17 (Cumulative), 3.79 (Last 60 Hours)
  - Elected or took team leader role in every group setting this year
  - Extensive speaking and presentation experience; gave at least one presentation a week
  - 2nd Place in Best Pitch for UTSA's $100K Business Plan Competition
  - Finalist for UTSA's 100 Best Business Students - 2017
  - Dean's List – Fall 2016

- **SAN ANTONIO COLLEGE – Associate of Science**   Graduated December 2015
  - 3.46 (Graduation GPA)
  - Honor Roll – Fall 2010

OTHER SKILLS, AWARDS, AND QUALIFICATIONS

- National Merit Scholar – Commended
- Excellent computer skills: Word, PowerPoint, Excel, basic AutoCAD, hardware and software installation, computer maintenance and repair
- San Antonio Rugby Men's Team Captain – 2014 & 2015; Collegiate Rugby Team Captain – 2004 & 2015

15.

Open the Door with a Broadcast Letter
Instead of a Résumé

When cold calling a prospective employer, almost everyone sends a résumé with a cover letter. According to my mentor and career search expert Brook Carey, you can stand out and engage more if you initially use a Broadcast Letter instead of a résumé. This is a marketing piece, a teaser to solicit interest and start a dialogue. It's in a narrative format, not a bullet format, which basically says:

- This is what type of work I'm looking for
- These are some reasons why you should hire me
- This is what I think I can accomplish when I work for you
- I'd like to come in and talk to you or send you a résumé,

If a hiring manager or recruiter likes what she sees, she will ask you to send a résumé with more details. This allows you to establish a dialogue where you are talking with each other.

If you send a résumé as your initial contact, they can say, *"I've reviewed your résumé, thanks, we'll call if we are interested in the future."* You're shut down. There is nothing to talk about in a follow up conversation without appearing desperate.

The Broadcast Letter gives them something to respond to if they are interested, a next step. It gives you an opportunity to engage with your prospective employer, and when you do meet, you will be ready to wow them!

➔ TAKEAWAY — Look for ways to start a dialogue with potential employers, so they can't say, *"Thanks, we have your résumé, we'll call when we need someone like you."* A broadcast letter is one way to accomplish that if you do go the cold calling route.

- Use a Broadcast Letter instead of a résumé when cold calling a company.

- Format it to pique interest of the recruiter.

- Use it to open dialogue with a company you want to work for.

Now that you are armed with all the tools of the job-hunting trade, it's time to go out and meet your prospective employer face-to-face!

SECTION 3

NETWORK YOUR WAY TO YOUR DREAM JOB

By far the easiest way to find and land a job is to network yourself into the position before most job seekers even know the opening exists! Yet networking is a skill you just are never taught! Half of all job postings are never listed on the job boards; instead the positions are filled by candidates known to the hiring manager. To get known by prospective employers, get ready to network.

In Section 3, you will learn all about networking your secret weapon:

- How to become a master networker — Chapter 16
- Secrets to networking to find the job you want — Chapter 17
- How to master the secrets of networking — Chapter 18
- How to create an effective Elevator Pitch — Chapter 19
- Where and how to find the right job opening — Chapter 20
- How to network your way to the interview — Chapter 21

16.

Become a Master Networker

The Importance of Knowing Your Future Employer

The best way to get a job is to get to know your future employer by networking. You need to become a master networker to maximize your chance of career success.

There's a dirty little secret no one will tell you. The vast majority of new employees are hired because of someone they know. So your challenge is to get out in the market and get to know potential employers and influencers BEFORE you contact them about a job.

Hiring an employee is a risk for the hiring manager and the company overall. The hiring decision maker is putting her reputation on the line by choosing you. The company is going to spend a great deal of time and money interviewing candidates, onboarding the new employee, and providing costly training along with salary and benefits. The hiring manager needs to feel comfortable and reassured that she is making the right decision. The best and least risky hiring choice is to hire someone she already knows and trusts, someone she knows to be reputable, professional, hardworking, serious and responsible. So you need to get to know the hiring decision maker or influencer IN PERSON before the job even comes available, so you will have the best shot at being hired.

> **People hire people they know, not strangers. It reduces the risk and makes it easy to gain a sense of comfort with their hiring decision.**
> --Diane Huth – Superhero Branding --

Many jobs are never posted online or in public. These are offered to someone known by the hiring manager. This is common for many companies, but especially small companies without huge HR departments. You may find out about the job directly at a Board meeting or networking luncheon, or you may be offered the job directly by the hiring manager, or you may be invited to send in an application. In big companies, you probably will be asked to submit your résumé through an online portal where all job openings are posted, but your application will get the fast track and preference if you know the hiring manager.

It's Not WHAT You Know, It's WHO You Know That Matters

References and recommendations by your mentors frequently are the key to standing out from the competition and being the one person selected. Use every tool you have available, and network professionally and consistently, for the greatest possibility of success.

My son Alex is a case in point. I encouraged him to get internships beginning at the end of his freshman year of college. He had great SAT scores and class ranking, awards for high school football, leadership and scholastics, and steady work experience with Best Buy and Geek Squad for several years. But how could he cut through the clutter early in college to get any kind of engineering internship, much less a paid one? He couldn't get one on his own merits, because all paid internships would go to upcoming seniors or grad students with better college credentials.

So he started networking. He posted on Facebook that he was looking for an engineering internship, and I shared it with my network. And he sent emails with his résumé to a number of family friends who were well-positioned senior executives. His godfather Bob was the CEO of a leading marine services company based out of New York and Houston, but what were the chances of finding an internship in San Antonio for such a junior person?

Bob replied stating that Alex should send a résumé to his business email, and nothing happened. Then about 2 weeks later Alex received a call from a corporate Human Resources manager saying he was to report for work the following Monday to an almost unknown explosives engineering subsidiary of Bob's company located in San Antonio, of all places. He said, *"You mean show up for an interview?"* And she replied, *"No, you have the job, you just need to show up for work and fill out the paperwork there at the office."* They had two other interns that summer, but he got the job simply because of the personal relationship with the right person. That's the power of personal networking.

More recently, I decided I wanted to teach at the university level. I looked in the online job boards and found that a leading private university had an opening for an Adjunct Professor of Marketing. Just by chance, more than ten years ago, I had served on a volunteer committee for a new program in the Marketing Department of that same school. I emailed the head of the committee to see if he was still at the school. It turned out he is now the head of the Marketing Department, and the hiring decision maker. He told me to upload my résumé on the school's job board, and within a week I was notified that I had been hired. There was no interview, because he knew me and my professionalism and skills, so it was a low risk decision for him.

About the same time, another opening for an Adjunct Marketing Professor opened at a major state university in San Antonio. I knew the former head of the Marketing Department through the AMA (not to mention that we had been classmates in graduate school forty years previously.) He had just retired, but I asked him to put in a good word for me with the new department head who was being hired from out of state to take over his job. Several weeks later, I was called in for the interview, and hired within the week. I had the credentials for the job, of course, but the key thing was the recommendation of someone who was known and trusted. It reduced the hiring risk, and made it an easier decision than hiring someone without a personal recommendation.

My "adopted" son Ryan just landed a fabulous job at a major financial institution, based in great part due to the recommendation by an uncle of his who worked there. He made sure Ryan's résumé got to the right hiring manager. That often is all the difference it takes. Recommendation from a company employee is often the best endorsement you can have.

These are personal examples of how you can leverage personal and professional relationships to network yourself to your dream job.

4 Secrets to Getting to Know Your Future Employer

Here are 4 tips for forming relationships with any potential employer:

1. **Affinity**

    First and foremost, employers hire people who are LIKE THEM. It's a matter of AFFINITY. At a subconscious level, you are most open and receptive to people who are like you, who look like you, and act like you, and dress like you, and talk like you, and who went to the same school, or served in the same branch of the military. It's a series of shared common bonds that make it easy to connect at a personal level. That's why going to college alumni events, networking through your church, meeting people in a volunteer role, or participating in a shared activity is so important — it allows you to create affinity bonds.

2. **Likeability**

    Secondly, people hire people they LIKE. Likeability is a key attribute to cultivate when looking for a job — and for everything you do in life. You must be friendly, sociable, smile, shake hands, be sincere, be caring, and honestly enjoy life with gusto and be passionate about the work you do. Negative emotions like unhappiness, pessimism, cynicism, depression, anger, and hostility are instantly transmitted to people around you at a subconscious level — they follow you like a dark cloud and contaminate everyone you meet. They make you unlikeable — and that's a job killer. Change your outlook on life, or put the negative behind you to achieve career success. You can't fake it, so change it.

3. **Visibility**

People like and relate with people in the limelight. So it's important to DO THINGS that portray you publicly in a positive light. This includes volunteering to help others, serving on the Board of a professional association, becoming a speaker at a special event, gaining recognition by blogging or writing for a journal or magazine, or otherwise actively engaging in activities that will make you visible to your potential employer.

4. **Frequency of Contact**

I've learned a relationship secret: if you see a person in the same place or event multiple times, you automatically consider them to be a friend, whether or not you speak or introduce yourself. The first time you show up at a given place or event, you are a stranger. The third or fourth time you see each other in the same context, you nod and say "Hi". By the fifth or sixth time, you say "Hi" and interact in a friendly way — just by being in the same place at multiple times, you automatically become friends. Try it out at the health club, the library, a bookstore, a bar, a club, or Starbucks. You can further your career by getting known in this natural way by joining your trade association and going to all the events, consistently attending networking events, or going to lunches or dinners where your potential employers congregate. So it's important that you get out and spend time where the career decision makers can be found on a consistent basis.

→ TAKEAWAY — People hire people they know and like, so you have to find ways to meet your potential employer, and connect on a personal level to use affinity to create an emotional bond.

To Do List

- Embrace the reality that your career success will depend on learning to network effectively, both on a personal and professional level.

- Now is the time to get rid of negativity and embrace positivity in your personal and professional life. Negative emotions, anger, resentment, and disparagement of others will affect how you are perceived by others. Get help if you need it, but change how you face the challenges and outcomes of your actions to positively influence how you are perceived by everyone you meet.

17.

Network to Find the Job You Want

The best way to meet and connect with your future employers is to join organizations where you will meet, interact with and serve with them. There are many different types of organizations, and you should belong to and participate in at least 4 of these types of organizations:

1. Industry professional or trade association
2. Target employer's industry association
3. Alumni association
4. Affinity group
5. Civic organization
6. Skills development organization

Here is the primer on how to network your way to your dream job.

1. <u>Join a Professional or Trade Association That Serves Your Functional Area or Profession</u>

First you need to join your professional associations — there may be one or several in your market. These are the associations for people in your field of work. If you work in marketing and advertising, you need to belong to the local chapters of the American Marketing Association (AMA), The American Advertising Federation (AAF), and perhaps the Public Relations Society of America (PRSA.) Certain cities may have purely local professional organizations as well — in Los Angeles and New England, it's the Ad Club, for example. If you are a banker, there are at least 16 different national banking associations. More than 25 associations serve the cybersecurity industry, 30 for higher education, 45 for biologists, 100 for nursing — you get the idea. Just google *"<industry name> professional associations,"* and you will find a comprehensive list of the associations that serve your industry.

If you're not a member of your key associations, join them right now — it's the best investment you will make in your career. Membership often costs between $100 and $200 per year, but you might be eligible for discounted student or associate memberships.

Surprisingly, I've found relatively little overlap between groups that serve the same industry. For many years, I belonged to both The American Marketing Association and the Advertising Federation, and I was surprised that there was relatively little crossover between groups – no more than 20%. Ad Fed was comprised of people who worked in ad agencies, website building, graphic design, media sales and printer and paper vendors. The AMA was comprised primarily of company marketing personnel, public relations, and some small agencies. So don't be afraid to join multiple organizations. Go to several meetings and events as a guest first to get the feel of each organization to make sure it is a fit with your professional interests.

2. Join Industry Associations That Serve Your Target Employer

If you work in manufacturing or finance, and you want a professional job with Frito-Lay, you might want to join the national Snack Food Association. If your career field is marketing and you want a job working for a bank, then join the local Bankers Association where you will meet employees of the different local banks. If you are an accountant, and want to work for a real estate broker, join the local real estate association. You will learn about your chosen industry, and meet the influencers and potential employers who will help you land your dream job.

3. Network Through Your Alumni Association

One of the very best ways to network is through your college's alumni association. They can give you a list of all the alumni in your city or state, along with contact information. They may have an online database of alumni you can search by city, state, industry, employer, past employers, job title, and more.

Join the social media pages of your school and your school alumni association — focus on Facebook and LinkedIn. You can reach out through a post saying *"I really want to work in project management for XYZ Corporation. Can you help me reach the hiring manager for the local office?"* You'll be amazed at the response.

Most local alumni associations offer local events or socials; attend as many as possible. If there is no local alumni association where you live, start one. It's easy; just call the alumni office and tell them where you live and offer to start a local chapter. They will send you a whole packet of information, along with the database of all alumni in the region. Then email and call everyone on the list and ask to meet after work at 5:30 or 6:00 p.m. on a weekday at a bar or restaurant for a networking social or dinner. You will have an immediate bond with other alumni due to the power of affinity. You can set up your alumni contact database using Mail Chimp to send out email invites, and manage your invitations to attend and reservations on an EventBrite page.

4. <u>Network Through Affinity Groups</u>

You can bond with others who have things in common with you as a fun and natural way of building your network. Join organizations that bring you in close touch with people who have something in common with you.

These may be based on items outside your control like gender, race, ethnicity, age, or physical traits. There are African-American organizations like NAACP, National Black Nurses Association, and the National Black MBA Association. Latinos might want to join LULAC, National Society of Hispanic Journalists, US Hispanic Chamber of Commerce, or National Association of Hispanic Real Estate Professionals. Women should consider organizations like NAWBO (National Association of Women Business Owners), WIB (Women in Business), AAUW (American Association of University Women), AWC (Association of Women in Communications), or Zonta International. There are clubs for redheads — RANGA (Red & Nearly Ginger Association), League of Redheads, National Association for the Advancement of Red Headed People, International Red Heads Society — who would have guessed? Depending on your height, you can join TCI (Tall Clubs International) or National Organization of Short Statured Adults or Little People of America. If you are in the top 2% of IQ, join MENSA and go to their local and national events. The number of groups you can join to meet and network with similar people is almost infinite – so join a few you will enjoy.

Affinity can also be based on interests and activities. Join any club for hiking, ice skating, new moms, wine lovers, gardeners, astronomy buffs, and more. Join MeetUp online, create your profile, and you can find hundreds of local activity-based groups for any kind of interest. If you have a hobby or interest that's not listed, start one — you will immediately become well known in the local market.

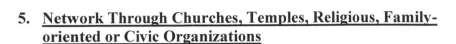

5. Network Through Churches, Temples, Religious, Family-oriented or Civic Organizations

All religious organizations are great ways to network. So are organizations that support your family members — PTA, band boosters, or athletic boosters for school organizations, Cub Scouts and Girl Scouts, and hundreds more.

Many civic or service organizations are dedicated to doing good for the community, and often their members and volunteers tend to be professionals with great contacts.

Rotary Clubs are active business organizations that many corporate leaders belong to. Similar service organizations include Kiwanis, Lions Clubs, Junior League, DeMolay and Masons, etc. Some of these organizations tend to have much older members, but the CEO or VP or owner of your target company may belong, and you would definitely stand out as a young member. Younger people tend to volunteer for organizations like Habitat for Humanity that are activity based. Consider volunteering for a political party or campaign — you will meet many passionate inspired people there! The key is that people who volunteer for civic organizations tend to be mid-to-high-level professionals who are active and engaged in the community, well connected, and may introduce you to the right person to land your job.

6. Network Through Skills Development Organizations

Last, but not least, there are organizations that help you develop or improve your skills. Toastmasters helps you master public speaking. Join MeetUp groups that will teach you social media skills or dozens of other professional skills. And of course your professional trade associations provide valuable information, education, and networking opportunities.

Volunteer to Really Connect

Often, when people go to a networking event, they stand in a corner and nobody talks to them; then they think, *"That wasn't any fun,"* and they go home without any benefit from the event or the organization. While it is important to attend networking events, the way to really get to know other people is to volunteer. Sign up for a committee, or get a seat on the Board. Organizations are always looking for volunteers.

Before I knew all about networking, I occasionally attended American Marketing Association luncheons and never really engaged with anyone. I felt alone and left out and didn't attend regularly. Then one day the president said, *"Hey, I need somebody to handle Public Relations. Can you do PR?"* I said, *"Sure, I can handle PR, I guess."* With that, I joined the Board, became involved, met everybody in the marketing community and showcased my talents to my peers. I was no longer on the sidelines; I was in the inner circle.

When you're on a Board or committee, you're on the inside and in the know. You know all the gossip first. You're the one who is recognized in the newsletter. You get to stand up and introduce yourself at the luncheons. But most importantly, you know everything that's happening in your industry. You will often hear about job openings in your field before they are ever made public. At a monthly Board meeting, one of your colleagues may say, *"Did you know Mary just took a new job at XYZ Company?"* You just learned there is now an opening at her old company. You can call Mary to get information on the job, the company, contact information, and maybe even a referral to someone at the company if she left in good standing. All this can happen before the company can even post the job opening on *Monster*! With networking, you can get your foot in the door before anyone else even knows about the job opening.

Three Key Volunteer Committees to Advance Your Goals

Volunteering to do something for your organization is very important. I have three favorite volunteer positions that I strongly recommend if you are looking to network, meet people and hopefully find a new job: Hospitality, Membership and Public Relations.

1. Hospitality Committee

The Hospitality Committee is responsible for making members feel at home, connecting with other people, and basically ensuring they have a positive experience at the event or with the organization. So whenever Joanne attends your organization's event for the first time, you get to go over and say, *"Hello, Joanne, I see you're a new member. Welcome. I'm Diane and*

I work for XYZ Company. What do you do?" You can ask questions like, *"Is there anyone in particular you'd like to meet today?"* and *"Tell me a bit about your business."* So now she is talking and you are learning about her.

Then you get to do matchmaking based on the information you just learned by introducing people to each other: *"Joanne, I'd like to introduce you to Robert, who works in your same industry. Why don't you sit with him and you can discuss what's happening in your industry?"* Joanne is grateful to you, because she is no longer standing around by herself thinking *"Nobody's talking to me."* Robert is grateful because you just brought him a potential customer or colleague. They both think you are wonderful, and they both owe you a favor. It's that simple to connect with two new people through your volunteer role. And of course if Joanne is someone you want to meet, or who works for your target company, you ask her to sit with you!

Some organizations don't have a hospitality function. No problem — volunteer to start a Hospitality Committee. In essence, you are creating your own volunteer role. Do a web search to find out best practices for Hospitality Committee members, and it will be easy to make an immediate difference in the organization — while you meet and make friends with everyone.

2. <u>Membership Committee</u>

The second opportunity is to volunteer for the Membership Committee. It's more work than Hospitality, but a secret source of opportunity for a job seeker. The Membership Committee is responsible for selling memberships to new members, and is responsible for making sure all current members renew. That gives you access to the entire database of your organization, so you will know who everyone is and who they work for and you will have access to their contact information. As a general rule, you're not allowed to use the database for personal gain or business use. So you can't download the list and use it to try and sell something to people on the list. However, now you have an excuse to call up the president of a company you want to work with and say, *"Hello, Mr. Jones. I'm calling from the AMA. I see that your membership is renewing in March. Could I come by your office for 15 minutes to update you on the benefits of membership and discuss upcoming programs?"* There is practically no other way you can connect with leaders in your industry as comfortably and easily as this.

3. <u>Public Relations Committee</u>

The PR Committee is generally responsible for publishing press releases, news bulletins and calendar alerts about the organization and its events. You might also end up writing a newsletter or setting up media interviews. This is your opportunity to build your personal brand visibility, because your name will be on every press release you send to the media, that will then be picked up by Google search. It's also a very effective way to create or gain access to a media database of journalists that you may end up contacting for a personal or business story. And it generally doesn't take too much of a time investment.

→ TAKEAWAY — There are hundreds of different organizations you can use to build your personal network. Then get involved and volunteer for a committee or board position to get engaged and well-known within the organization.

- Research, visit, then join at least 4 different organizations that will allow you to rapidly expand your professional and personal network:

  - Industry professional or trade association
  - Target employer's industry association
  - Alumni association
  - Affinity group
  - Civic organization
  - Skills development organization

- Make a commitment to attend events and activities each and every month — membership will not help you if you don't show up.

- Then volunteer to serve on a committee or the Board to become an industry insider.

18.

Master the Secrets of Networking

Now that you have joined several organizations, you have to show up and participate!

Most organizations have weekly or monthly luncheons, and a couple of evening networking socials throughout the year, in addition to workshops and seminars. Some groups feature breakfast meetings, others evening dinners or cocktail events. Join organizations that fit into your lifestyle so it will be easy and convenient to attend the events. Attend whenever possible, and actively network with the others in the room.

How I Learned the Secret of Successful Networking

When I moved to San Antonio from Florida fifteen years ago, I knew nobody. I was a recently divorced single woman, and I didn't know a soul. I sat at home for a few months because I didn't know how to connect with other people. Then somebody from my homeowners' association said, *"Hey, there's a big party for a local charity this weekend; here's an invitation."* I decided I had to change my life as I was miserable and alone and lonely, so I made up my mind to go — by myself.

I sat in the car in my evening gown outside the event center, terrified to walk into a room full of hundreds of strangers by myself. I finally got up the nerve, walked in the door, stuck out my hand and said *"Hi, I'm Diane, and I'm a new Texan."* I repeated this introduction all night long. I met dozens of people, and everyone was friendly and welcoming. I had a wonderful time and I danced until 1:30 in the morning. Then, just the next week, I ran into a couple of those same people at a restaurant, joined them at their table, and they weren't strangers any more. All of a sudden I had a wonderful group of friends. In the years since, it has snowballed until I have a huge personal and online network of friends and business colleagues. If I had not put aside my fear (terror is more like it) and walked into that room full of strangers and started introducing myself, my life would have taken a very different course. Yours will too when you master the art of networking.

How to Work the Room at a Networking Event

The goal at networking events is to network. So don't hang around or sit with your friends or sit at a table full of students from your school or colleagues from your office. Actively seek out new people you don't know, and ask to sit with them.

Force yourself out of your comfort zone and actively seek to meet new people. Shake hands, and say *"Hi, I'm Diane, and I'm brand new here,"* or *"Hi, I'm the PR Chair for this organization and I don't think I have met you before,"* or *"Hi, I belonged to this organization in Houston, but I just moved here and am looking forward to meeting other members like you."* Then, sit at a table of strangers. Always sit at a table with people you don't know, because at the end of the event, they're going to be your friends

or at least acquaintances. How are you going to meet people if you don't sit with them and talk to them? You have to force yourself out of your comfort zone and actively reach out to new people.

Master the Art of Shaking Hands

Next, you need to master the all-important hand shake. No wimpy finger shakes, ladies, and no crushing of fingers, guys. When you say your name, stick out your right hand, insert your hand securely into the other person's hand thumb-to-thumb and palm-to-palm. Firmly grasp the offered hand, look the person you are greeting in the eye, smile, shake hands 3 times, then release.

To be really sincere or intimate, use the two-hand shake. Look the person in the eye, and grasp the offered hand firmly with your right hand, and then clasp the back side of the person's hand with your left hand, and shake. Release your left hand first, then release your right hand. I would recommend using this sparingly, as you don't want to be known as a groper, but it can be good for a very special person or relationship.

Wear Your Nametag on Your RIGHT Shoulder

Nametags are essential for networking. Most organizations will have preprinted computer-generated stick-on nametags for networking events. Sometimes you will receive a blank adhesive nametag and a Sharpie pen to write your own name tag. Practice writing an attractive nametag, with your first name large and very visible, and your last name underneath a bit smaller. If you want to add your company name, it should be centered at the bottom in a smaller size printing.

Even better, you can invest $10 or $15 to create your own permanent nametag. If you currently don't have a job, list your profession instead of company — what you aspire to do. For example: Marketing, Accounting, Human Resources, Writer-Editor, IT, Database Management, Auto Repairs, etc. Don't put your school name if you are still in school. And never put intern, job seeker, or unemployed on anything!

You wear your nametag on your RIGHT shoulder, just below your collarbone, about where you would put your hand to say the pledge of allegiance on the other shoulder. You want your name tag to be seen when you introduce yourself to someone. When you stick out your right hand to shake hands, your right shoulder will roll forward, and your name tag will be clearly visible. When you shake hands, your left shoulder rolls backwards, and the person you are meeting can't see your nametag well if it is on the left shoulder.

Manage Giving and Receiving Business Cards

Presenting, accepting, and managing business cards is an art. I keep my business cards in the left pocket of my jacket, always within easy reach. You don't want to be fumbling in your purse or wallet for a card — that's awkward and distracting. When I meet someone I want to give a business card to, I dip my left

hand into my left pocket and pull out a card while I am reaching out with my right hand to shake hands. Then I present my card so that it is facing the recipient and not upside down. At that point, the recipient feels obligated to return the gracious gesture, and he gives me one of his cards.

Take the offered card in both hands, read it, say the name, and thank the giver for the card. Then slip it into your RIGHT side pocket. In this way, you aren't fumbling through many cards to find one of yours, and you aren't giving away a card with a hand-written note on the back. Practice this before your next networking event so it comes to you naturally. Remember, your cards in your left pocket, and their cards in your right pocket.

Business card etiquette is very different in different countries and cultures, so study up on the cultural nuances before traveling overseas.

Learn My 3-Person Rule

I have a networking rule cast in stone: every time you go out to an event of any kind, you must meet and really connect with 3 people. You can't leave until you have spoken one-on-one with 3 people, found out where they work, what they do, what their hobbies are, how long they've belonged to the association or have been attending their events. And you must exchange business cards — that one with your photo, remember? Three new people should be your mantra.

So every time you network, you don't need to meet everybody. You just have to really meet and get to know just 3 people. It's not overwhelming when you focus on just 3 people. At the end of the year, you will know at least 36 new people well from just one group that meets monthly. Those people will introduce you to their friends to  exponentially expand your network. Then all of a sudden you will walk into a room full of friends instead of strangers.

Introduce Yourself Memorably

 Most people don't know how to introduce themselves. They say their name as if is just one word. *"Hi, I'm Barbarajacobson."* The person you are meeting can't understand what you just said. They hear *"Hi, I'm Barbara blah blah blah."* You need to put an auditory space between your first and last name so it can be heard, processed, understood and then hopefully remembered. You must learn that you have a new middle name and it is SPACE. So when you introduce yourself, you say, *"Hi, I'm Barbara (space) Jacobson."* You need to practice it until it flows smoothly and naturally. There's a great TED Talk that demonstrates this: *Want to sound like a leader? Start by saying your name right* - by Laura Sicola of TEDxPenn.

Look for and try to create an auditory prompt so your name is easy to remember. If you have a name with another meaning, try using it as a memory prompt. My friend Brook Carey introduces herself by saying *"Hello, I'm Brook Carey. That's Brook like a babbling brook, and Carey like Mariah Carey."* They will

remember her name because she created a rich visual image in their mind, and a visual image is stronger than just an auditory message for creating memory. I have an unusual last name, so I introduce myself on the phone as *"Hi, I'm Diane Huth — that's H-U-T-H Huth."* In the past I tried to add, *"It's pronounced Huth — like Ruth."* That was memorable — but everyone remembered *Ruth* instead of *Diane* and called me *Ruth*, so that didn't work out so well. Your challenge is to come up with a clever way to help a stranger remember your name, and practice your introduction until it comes naturally.

It's Important to Remember THEIR Names

You must also remember and repeat the name of the person you just met. Repeat the new person's name at least three times in the first minute after an introduction to help remember his name. Your conversation might go. *"Hi, Steve, it's nice to meet you. Steve, what do you do for a living? Steve, I want to introduce you to my friend Mary. Mary, this is Steve, Steve, this is Mary."* At the end of this exchange, you will probably remember that his name is *"Steve."*

My Secret Name Recall Tip

Remembering someone's name is very important in creating likeability. But sometimes you do forget. Let me share my secret trip for recalling someone's name.

For several years, I headed up both a trade organization and a singles social group, and was on the podium presenting speakers and addressing the audience at events. Many people knew my name, but I didn't know or remember theirs. Like many people, I'm awful at remembering names in the first place, so it was a real challenge for me. I created this technique that will serve you well in your career.

When someone comes up to me and says *"Hi, Diane, I haven't seen you in ages,"* I don't ask them who they are — that would be an insult. Instead I immediately shake hands and then introduce them to someone whose name I do know. The conversation might go like this: *"I'm great, thanks. I'd like to introduce you to my friend Bob."* Bob politely sticks out his hand and says *"Hi, I'm Bob Jones."* Then the new person introduces herself to Bob, saying, *"Hi, Bob, I'm Barbara*

Jacobson." Aha! Now I know her name, and I can say *"Barbara, what have you been up to lately?"*

It's All About Them

When you're talking to people while you are networking, there is one golden rule: *"It's not about you, it's about them."* Being a good conversationalist doesn't mean that you talk in an enchanting or interesting manner about yourself. It means that you LISTEN to them talk about themselves! They don't care about you, quite frankly. They want to talk about themselves and you may have to prompt them to get started.

Ask them about themselves, *"How long have you belonged to this organization?"* *"What do you do for a living?"* *"How long have you worked for that company?"* *"That's an interesting last name — what is the origin?"* *"What are your biggest challenges in your job today?"* Your challenge is to get them talking about themselves, their company and their interests. As they talk, you nod and give them words or gestures and body language of encouragement or acknowledgement. They're going to think you're fascinating. Ask smart questions. Every time you ask smart questions and they answer, you should acknowledge and affirm what they say with a nod, a smile, an *"umhumm"* or a statement of interest.

My friend and mentor John Carter told me how he was hired right out of graduate school for a much sought-after job in account management with the J. Walter Thompson advertising agency in New York City — a plum of a job. He had an on-campus interview with a recruiter, just like twenty other students that day. When he sat down with the recruiter, he said, *"I know what an account executive does, and I know what a copywriter does, but I don't know what Human Resources does."* The recruiter launched into an animated explanation of how important his job was and how business was changing and how they were the frontline for acquiring talent for the company and on and on. When the half-hour interview was over, John had never talked about himself or the job or his qualifications. He left discouraged — expecting another polite rejection letter. The company extended a job offer to only one person from that campus recruiting trip. Yep, John got the job — only because he was a good listener and got the interviewer to talk about himself.

Another of my friends has not been able to find a job despite great talent and experience. I took her with me to a professional networking social, and all she did was talk about herself all night long. I was talking with somebody whom I wanted to have come and speak at a class, and every time I asked him a question, she interrupted talking about herself and how she felt about the topic. I redirected the questions to him again and again, saying, *"Brad, tell me about this,"* and every time he tried to answer, she jumped in talking about herself and her opinions and experiences. I finally had to drag her away and say, *"Shut up. It's not about you, it's about him. Let him talk about himself and don't interrupt or talk about yourself."* She didn't know how to network effectively, and never really learned, which is why she still hasn't been able to land a job. So network wisely and effectively and listen much more than you talk. Set a goal of only talking ¼ of the discussion. You'll be amazed by how much you learn.

Follow Up Immediately After a Networking Event

At the end of any event, go home and send your 3 special new contacts a quick email before you go to bed. Don't wait until tomorrow or you will never get around to it. It can be something simple like *"It was such a pleasure to meet you tonight at the AMA social. I'd like to stay in touch. Perhaps we can connect on LinkedIn."* Immediately go to LinkedIn and send her an invitation. Then you can communicate and build on your relationship and set up that one-on-one meeting.

If you really are interested in the person or company, hand-write a thank you note with pen and paper. Handwriting a thank you note is an almost obsolete forgotten skill, but people respond to it, in part because they can't hit "delete" to make it go away. If you have bad handwriting, type the note nicely on a good linen paper or notecard stock, sign it and send it in the mail. The important thing is to reach out to the other person on paper, and insert or attach your business card (with your photo of course) as a tangible reminder of your meeting. This connection really is very powerful. You can say, *"I enjoyed hearing about your company last night. It sounds like you have fascinating opportunities. Could we get together and have a cup of coffee next week to learn more about it? I'd love to work for a company like yours."* It is that easy.

Master the Secret Art of Team Networking

One of the skills I have honed is that of Team Networking. My friend Marie Ferrante is a very good graphic designer and we attend professional networking events together. When I meet someone new, I introduce them to Marie with praise. *"It's a pleasure to meet you, John. I want to introduce you to my friend, Marie. She's the best graphic designer in town. She does all my graphic design work; and I've worked with her for ten years. I think you need to know each other."* Then Marie says *"Oh, it's so easy to do great work for someone like Diane. She is the most brilliant marketer I've ever met. She's introduced me to the most wonderful clients. I just love working with her."*

So we each bragged about each other! I didn't brag about myself, and Marie didn't brag about herself, right? But we told John a great deal of favorable information about each other. In this way, I can act modest because I bring my cheering squad with me, and we both look good Plus it's much more fun to go networking with a friend — especially if you have complementary or non-competing skills and aren't both looking for the same job.

Networking No-Nos

Some topics should be avoided at networking events. You should never talk about religion or politics. And never, ever talk negatively about anybody, including nasty people that you've worked with before or people you hate. That's private. Discussing it will make you look petty. Don't ever bring negative topics or experiences into a professional social networking event, or interview for that matter. And don't gossip or reveal secrets about a former employer, even if you left unhappily. You will be seen as being disloyal. After all, if you will tell me confidential information about your former employer, I have to assume you would probably do the same if you end up working for my company.

➔ TAKEAWAY — Networking is your secret weapon to landing a great job. People prefer to hire people they know. So your challenge is to effectively network and meet both the people who can refer you to a job, as well as your future employer through industry and civic associations. Network your way to your dream job!

To Do List

- Practice shaking hands effectively and smiling, while introducing yourself memorably by saying your name slowly, with a space between your first and second name

- Practice your opening line — how you introduce yourself, and what memory-stimulating device you will use

- Practice exchanging business cards, keeping your cards in your left pocket and their cards in your right pocket

- Order a permanent name tag from your local trophy shop; make a note to always wear it on your right shoulder

- Find a friend with whom you can team network

19.

Master Your Elevator Pitch

One of the key skills you need to develop before you start actively networking is your Elevator Pitch.

Picture yourself in New York City, and you're in the elevator going to the 56th floor, and you walk on to the elevator and the man you've always wanted to meet and work for is standing right there next to you in the elevator. You have just 30 seconds to make a great impression on him and ask him for an appointment or an interview. What are you going to say in those critical 30 seconds?

That's your Elevator Pitch. It's your 30-second ad that will tell him who you are, what you can do for him, provide proof that you can do it, and ask him for the interview.

It's not something you can make up on the spot. It's a carefully crafted 4 or 5 sentence sales pitch that you create, wordsmith until it's perfect, and practice until you can deliver it almost without thinking about it. It must feel and sound natural and unrehearsed and enthusiastic.

You must figure out what you want to say in 30 seconds to land the appointment, because it only takes 30 seconds to get to the 56th floor.

There are only 4 key elements of an Elevator Pitch:

1. **Introduction**

   First you introduce yourself audibly and memorably — remember "space" is your middle name: *"Hi, Ellen, I'm Diane (space) Huth. I'm the author of Brand YOU! to Land Your Dream Job."* Give her an audio cue if necessary so she can remember your name.

2. **What You Do**

   Tell her what you do for others or what you can do for her. *"I help job-seekers create a comprehensive and compelling self-branding program with a step-by-step guide so they can find and land their dream job."* Other examples might be:

- *"I work with small businesses to solve their legal issues before they become problems."*
- *"I work with at-risk teenagers to help them find their path in life and avoid drugs, crime and teen pregnancy."*
- *"I help businesses create brilliant advertising to help them achieve and surpass their sales goals."*
- *"I'm a marketing strategist and troubleshooter and I love solving branding problems so that you can increase your brand's preference and adoption by your target customers."*

3. Proof of Value

Next, you provide proof of value, to prove that you can do what you say you can do. *"Ellen, I have trained more than 2,000 graduating college students using my Brand YOU! Program, and they have an impressive 88% hire rate within three months after taking my class."* Other examples might be:

- *"I just finished a consulting assignment with XYZ Bank where I helped them reposition their credit card products, and they increased new applications by 20% in just 3 months."*
- *"My company has filmed 35,000 birth videos in the last year."*
- *"I've just completed an internship with XYZ company where I was responsible for all social media, and I created a promotion that drove 5,000 new Likes on Facebook."*
- *"I've been on the Board of the AMA for the last seven years, and helped the organization grow by fifteen percent in the first four months."*

4. Call to Action

This is when you ask for what you want — the specific action you hope to achieve. *"Ellen, I'd like to come on your show and share tips on managing your social media presence to help job seekers get found and hired by recruiters and employers."* Other calls to action might include:

- *"I would like to learn more about your company. Could you spare fifteen minutes in the next week so I could come by and learn more about your organization?"*
- *"It sounds like just the kind of company I've always wanted to work for. Could you join me for a cup of coffee to talk more about your company and the job opportunities in your department?"*
- *"You're doing exactly what I want to do when I graduate. Would it be possible to shadow you at work for a day to learn more about the realities of this profession?"*

- *"I have always wanted to work for your company. Could you introduce me to the hiring manager in the finance department?"*

Here are some examples of Elevator Pitches for different industries. More samples are available on BrandYouGuide.com:

Hello, I'm Alex Myers, and I'm currently a senior studying Computer and Information Science. I hope to become a computer programmer when I graduate this December. I've had three 3 internships where I worked on multiple program applications with project teams. I enjoy tackling difficult programs and creating a simple and easy-to-implement solution for small businesses. The position you have listed on the Job Board seems like it would be a perfect fit for someone with my skills. I'd like to hear more about the type of project teams in your organization.	Hi, my name is Roberta Rodriguez, and I am a business major at Texas A&M University with a concentration in International Marketing. I'm looking for a position that will allow me to use my native Spanish language skills and my business education to help grow your business in Latin America. I have benefited from an internship working for a solar energy company to help plan their service launch in Costa Rica and Peru. Eventually, I'd like work in marketing and product management in Latin America for a company like yours. Could you introduce me to your VP of International Marketing so we could discuss your current Latin American programs to see how I might be able to contribute to your growth plans?
Hello, Dr. Jamison, I am Nancy Barnes, an OBGYN nurse at St. Mary's Hospital. I have more than 10 years experience in Obstetrics and Emergency Room nursing, and was responsible for opening 3 new OB clinics for University Hospital in Dallas before moving here. I have a BSN degree and am a certified nurse midwife. I understand you will be opening a new Obstetrics unit at your hospital this quarter, and I would love to be considered for a lead position on your team. Could I speak with you next week to learn about the specific needs for your upcoming program, and discuss my experience and skills?	I am John Robertson, a freelance graphic designer based in Houston. I specialize in graphic design, logo design and printed corporate branded materials such as brochures, business stationery and websites, and more. I offer you innovative and effective design solutions that will help you grow your business. Having worked for 15 years in New York and Chicago, I boast an diverse client base that includes more than 20 Fortune 500 companies and brands. I offer competitive rates, quick turn around and a satisfaction guarantee. Can I have 15 minutes of you time to show you my portfolio?

Right Now, Stop and Write Your Elevator Pitch:

Take 10 minutes right now to write down and fine tune your Elevator Pitch. Remember, there are just 4 simple sequential parts to get your message across concisely and persuasively.

Introduction:

_____

What You Do or Offer:

_____

_____

Proof of Value:

_____

_____

Call to Action:

_____

Practice Your Elevator Pitch Until It Comes Naturally

After you have your Elevator Pitch drafted, you must practice it until it rolls off your tongue without thinking about it. When you meet Mr. Big in that elevator, you can't fumble in your pocket and say, *"Let me look for my Elevator Pitch."* You can't pull it up on the computer. You have to nail it right then and there in person. You need to practice it and memorize it until it feels natural. Seriously, you should practice your Elevator Pitch at least 100 times before you need it. Pitch yourself in the bathroom mirror every morning and night. Pitch it to the toilet paper dispenser in the bathroom. Practice it while driving in the car or microwaving a cup of coffee — which will let you time it to exactly thirty seconds. Practice on family members, friends, colleagues, even the family dog — he'll never criticize it. Practice shaking hands, smiling into a mirror, and giving your Elevator Pitch until it comes so naturally that you find yourself using it without thinking about it.

Make Adjustments for Different Industries or Opportunities

Once you are comfortable with the basic pitch, you need to make minor adjustments to tailor it to the specific person you are talking to or the company you are pitching. And remember, it's really about them, not about you. You are trying to express why they should take their valuable time and interest to invest in you, so you need to show them how it is to their benefit to meet with you.

- If you've just met Mr. Big of AT&T, you would say, *"I've always wanted to work in the telecommunications industry for your company."*
- If you meet someone from an ad agency, you would tailor the pitch to say, *"I've always wanted to work in an ad agency. In fact, I've had the opportunity to work with some wonderful ad agencies during my 10-year career on the client side."*
- Or you can pique their interest by expressing knowledge about them or their company. *"I thought your company's recent acquisition of XYZ company was brilliant. I'd love to learn more about it from the perspective of someone who was intimately involved in the decision."*
- Or *"I understand you've been on the Board of this association for five years. Could you share with me how you feel it has helped you in your current job role?"*

These 30 seconds will change your career path and your professional life.

➜ TAKEAWAY —— Your Elevator Pitch is a key tool in your job-hunting arsenal, and you need to practice it until it comes rolling off your tongue without thinking about it. Only in this way will you be truly ready to take advantage of great opportunities when they land unexpectedly in your lap.

- Carefully craft your Elevator Pitch, and practice it over and over until it rolls off your tongue without thinking about it.

- Then (and only then) practice variations for different jobs, companies, industries or occasions.

20.

How to Find the Right Job Opening

By now, you have all your job-hunting tools ready to go, you have honed your networking skills, and you've mastered your Elevator Pitch. So it's time to find the job opening and get the interview.

Know Where the Jobs Are

If you are alive and breathing and looking for a job, you know all about the online career job boards. Some of the most popular ones are *Monster, CareerBuilder, Indeed, The Ladders* (higher level positions), *Simply Hired, Jobs.com,* and *Us.jobs* (government jobs.) Many temp firms, headhunters, and brick and mortar employment agencies also offer online job listings. *Glassdoor* additionally provides ratings of companies by current and former employees.

These job boards are the key way most job seekers look for a job. They all provide many job listings and search capabilities, and you should definitely register with at least one and perhaps several of them. You don't need to pay a fee, but some do provide premiums services that may be worth a small investment until you find that dream job.

Just as importantly, these often provide very valuable information and insights for job seekers, so you can benefit from their online resources, blogs, guides, and email newsletters loaded with tips and guidance.

The Online Job Application Black Hole

The problem is that everyone in the world can access the same jobs, so the competition is fierce. A company may receive thousands of applications for just one open position. The screening job is overwhelming for a person — so a computer does it instead. Your résumé must be formatted to precisely fit each job description or the computer will pass it by.

Job search sites use algorithms and key word searches just like Google does, so your résumé must be tailored to each application to mirror the language of the job. If the description lists "*QuickBooks*," or "*database management,*" or "*GIS*" or "*PMP certification,*" make sure you use the exact same terms on your résumé so the computer will match your résumé to the description.

I personally have never had much success submitting an application on any of the job search sites, but that doesn't mean they aren't a goldmine for a job seeker. I have a number of friends who have found great jobs online, so definitely use these resources.

Perhaps the most important use of the job boards is to identify a job you want, which then allows you to network your way to the job decision-maker so you stand out from the crowd. Then after you connect to the decision-maker, he will probably tell you to submit an online application so he can legally review it and hire you.

Most Jobs Are Never Listed on the Job Boards

Most of the jobs you find on the job boards are for large companies and institutions. But most open jobs are with small companies and never appear on the job boards. The Small Business Association (SBA) says that 67% of all net new jobs are for small companies with 2 to 500 employees. And an estimated 40% to 80% of all new jobs are never posted online. Hiring is often done by networking, by word of mouth, by ads in *Craig's List* or *Zip Recruiter* or the local newspaper. Many are listed through professional association job boards or alumni associations. Even if the big job boards pick up those listings, it may be weeks after the job was first opened, and you can already have positioned yourself as the best candidate by then.

Other Resources to Find the Perfect Job

The easy way to find out about a job opening is to wait until it appears listed on a job site. However, a much more effective way to find your dream job is to identify the company you want to work for, and then network your way to an interview. Here are some great resources to find the companies you want to work for, and then reach out to the right decision-makers in those companies:

- **LinkedIn**

  Use the Company search function to find people in key positions who currently or previously worked for your target company. You can search out people with secondary connections to your target employer and ask them to give you an introduction.

- **Your School Alumni Association**

  The Alumni Office of your college or university actively maintains a database of all alumni, and you usually can make an online search by geography, industry, company name, and other search criteria to find people currently or previously employed there.

- **The Directory of Associations**

  Go to http://www.DirectoryOfAssociations.com/ to find every imaginable trade and professional association. Search from there to find your desired field, and identify local chapters or local members.

- **Your Own Professional Associations**

  There are scores of different professional associations in the city where you live, and you benefit most by attending local meetings and events. You will network at events, and most associations also publish lists of members or member companies that you can reach out to directly.

- **The Book of Lists**

  Business Journals publishes a list of the top 20 companies in each different industry in 60 key US markets. It's a great source to identify potential employers. Go to *http://www.bizjournals.com/* and search for Book of Lists.

- **Chambers of Commerce**

  Every city has a number of different Chambers of Commerce, segmented by zone, interest, ethnicity, country of origin, and more. This is where you will find representatives of your key companies with local contact information.

- **Local Networking Groups**

  There are many local groups from Meet Up groups to Business Lead Exchanges and networking breakfast clubs. Get out and meet everyone you can. At many of the networking events, a substantial number of attendees will either be trying to sell you something or be unemployed and looking for a job, but be persistent and you will build your database of potential leads.

- **Rotary Clubs**

  There are a number of local Rotary Clubs in your city. This is a business group that holds weekly lunch, breakfast or dinner meetings, and operates many community charitable activities. What is so relevant is that they only accept one member from each industry, so you will meet a range of people at a given meeting. And company owners or senior executives generally belong to Rotary. Go to Rotary.com for information about local clubs.

- **Manufacturers' Associations**

Most cities have at least one professional association that serves the manufacturing community, and they will list member companies. You will be amazed to find so many local companies you never even heard of. The local organization will probably host an annual trade show, so walk the floor to learn about the companies in your area engaged in manufacturing. They often will have an online directory that will also be very valuable.

Google is your friend in this process — just google the type of organization you want to find, and you will receive a plethora of networking opportunities. I could literally go to a networking event every single day of the month for breakfast, lunch and dinner, so rest assured, you will never run out of opportunities to find potential employers.

Also, most large companies will have a link to a page on their website for *"Careers"* or *"Jobs"* or *"Employment."* Search there for openings and contact HR through that site.

Attend Every Job Fair You Can Find

If a company chooses to spend money renting a booth and sending their recruiters to a job fair, they are seriously interested in hiring new employees.

Set a Google Alert for *"Job Fair <Your City>"* to learn of upcoming events. Most job fairs are advertised in the newspaper, so check your online and printed newspapers. Most colleges also offer on-campus job fairs, so make sure you attend them as well. They are focused on entry-level positions, so recruiters expect to meet with upcoming graduates.

Research the list of companies that plan to attend, select those of interest, and personalize a copy of your résumé just for that company. Dress for success, bring a professional looking résumé and a striking business card with your photo. Connect with each recruiter; remember that it's all about them and the company's needs and not about you. Shake hands, offer your business card, and deftly deliver your Elevator Pitch. Ask for a follow-up interview. Ask for each recruiter's business card, as well as any brochures or printed literature they offer. And take many notes as you will forget key points and contact information if you don't capture it right then and there.

Immediately that same day, send a thank you email to all the recruiters you met, reminding them about a key point of your qualifications or discussion, and ask for a personal interview.

Also mail a follow up letter within 24 hours of the job fair, asking for the interview. Include your résumé and business card with your photo to prompt their memory.

If you don't get an interview or response right away, send a follow up email and make a phone call after 2 weeks. Then follow up with the recruiter by phone or email once a month to stay connected and see if something opens up at a later time.

➡ TAKEAWAY — There are many ways to find the companies that you want to work for. Don't wait for a job to be posted to apply. Cold call those companies, or network your way to an interview and you'll be hired before anyone even knows there's an opening.

To Do List

- Register on 1 or more career job boards, and build out your online resume and profile.

- Use the job boards to identify desirable openings, then network to the decision maker.

- Research to identify attractive companies for cold-calling even though many may not have an opening at the time.

- Attend every job fair you can find; research companies and personalize a resume for each company.

21.

Cold Call Your Way to the Interview

Despite all your networking activities, your dream job may be with a company where you don't have a personal contact — yet. That means you need to "cold call" them to get the interview.

Get Ready to Storm the Castle by Cold Calling

Once you know who you want to work for, but don't know anyone at the company, you need to start to "storm the castle." Companies today make it very difficult for job hunters to get in the door except through online job boards, from which you may never receive a response.

When I first moved to San Antonio 15 years ago, I had more than 20 years of stellar marketing experience, which included several years of telecommunications experience. AT&T was headquartered here at the time, and had 19 marketing positions posted online that I was qualified for. I did everything possible to get an interview, and in over a year of applying to their dozens of online job posts, I never received a single response in writing or by phone. I even went to their corporate headquarters and tried to speak with someone in HR, and was turned away in the lobby. They wouldn't even allow me to leave my résumé! I was told that they only accepted applications online. Despite submitting my application dozens of times over many months, I never got a single response and was never able to speak with a human being at the company about a job. So I know it is daunting and frustrating. Perhaps if I knew then what I am about to share with you now, I would have had more success.

Network Your Way into Your Target Company

After you have identified the company you want to work for, you need to launch an all-out campaign to connect with either the hiring manager or the HR manager who can move your application through the process. It is not easy, and requires lots of creativity, research and hard work.

Use all the networking resources we have discussed so far — professional associations, alumni groups, your own social media pages, and more. Ask for an introduction or referral from everybody you know. Send an email to your network of friends and mentors asking for help getting an introduction into the company, and follow it up with a phone call immediately afterward to key mentors to make sure they take a minute to respond or listen. Don't forget to post a request for an introduction to anyone in the company on your Facebook and Twitter pages, and on your college alumni social media pages.

Use LinkedIn to Find a Contact in Your Target Company

During this cold-calling process, LinkedIn is your most important tool. Go to the target company's LinkedIn page, and search for first and second degree connections. When you identify a connection, call and email them asking for an introduction or a personal meeting, or both.

Then search for employees in your desired department and in the HR department, and send them an invitation to connect. Search their contact information tab to find an email or phone number, and try to reach them by phone or email. Send them an InMail if you have a premium subscription.

Search the company profile and identify key executives, and write down their names. Search using filters like location, function and seniority. Contact all of them by email, InMail and phone until you connect. You can also research them on Google to learn about their professional activities – perhaps you will find a keynote talk at a  trade show, a new board seat, an industry award, or a news article where they are quoted. If you show up at the event, you can probably meet the VIP in person, and he will often graciously accept your card and agree to speak with you after the event. You can also mention those items in your cover letter or at a job interview.

Don't mail your résumé — mail your Broadcast Letter instead (refer to Chapter 15 for information on creating your Broadcast Letter). It's a marketing piece to serve as a teaser, so they hopefully will request your résumé, opening a dialogue.

When you do connect with anyone working in the company, ask for a 15-minute meeting at their office, or over a cup of coffee at Starbucks, or on a quick phone call. Use this foot-in-the-door contact to gain information about the company, gather names of potential contacts, and learn about key company issues or initiatives. At the meeting itself, present your Broadcast Letter and résumé, and ask for an introduction or referral to both the HR manager and the hiring manager if possible.

Use Both Email and Snail Mail

When cold calling, remember to use all your available tools. Emails are perishable; they get pushed to the bottom of the email list and sometimes lost forever — whereas a written letter becomes a problem that has to be dealt with. I get more than 200 emails a day. If I check an email on my mobile phone, it is marked as read and drops from my new message list — out of sight, out of mind. Emails are easily overlooked. However, if you send a printed letter on very nice, crisp, bond letterhead, it can't be deleted. This tangible piece of paper becomes a problem the reader has to do something with. The recipient can throw it away, but it's easier to just forward it to the HR manager with a scribbled note suggesting that they interview you. Bingo!

Start at the Top – and Work Your Way Down

If you are cold calling a company and don't know anyone there, start your contact at the top whenever possible. Write to the president of the company, the VP of your field, and the VP of Human Resources until someone responds with an interview. Look to find points of contact you can leverage whenever possible.

For example, I met the Founder and CEO of a major technology company located where I live. I attended several TED[X] Talks hosted at the company headquarters, and met him there 4 times over the past few years when he was attending with his two sons. He probably doesn't remember my name, but I can now contact him mentioning our prior meetings, and may even mention some personal connection. An exchange might include: *"Hello, Mr. Big. I had the pleasure of meeting you and your two sons at this year's TED[X] event. You have exciting things going on in your company — and I'd like to be a part of it and contribute to your ongoing success. Could I speak with you for a few minutes to learn about your needs and discuss how I can fit into your organization and make immediate contributions?"* From there, I could give him my Elevator Pitch, send my Broadcast Letter, and ask to submit my résumé to him. Of course it will probably be opened by his administrative assistant, who will send it to the VP of Human Resources. But it WILL be seen by the VP, and he WILL set up an appointment because it came from the CEO's office.

Don't stop there. Work your way down the ladder and contact everyone below the CEO who could help you get an interview — the CEO's assistant, other VPs, other people in HR, anyone who works in the department you want to work in, anyone in your alumni association or networking group.

<u>Employee Referral — the Most Common Way to Get Hired</u>

According to recruiting expert Dr. John Sullivan, the best way to get hired (based on the number of hires) is through an internal employee referral. Companies actively encourage their employees to refer potential employees, and many give cash bonuses for a successful referral. One of my former employers offered $1,000 for any successful referral of any employee who was hired and employed for at least three months. You are not being a bother by asking an employee in your target company to refer you to HR; rather you are doing them a favor by making them eligible for a referral bonus. So network with passion to reach any current employee and ask them about the company and then ask them to provide a referral to HR. It's a little-known secret — and can be a gold mine for both of you.

Cold calling is often challenging, but if you convert cold calling into networking, you can manage to storm the gates and get your résumé seen by the right person.

→ TAKEAWAY — When you're trying to find a job without a networking contact, use every resource, relationship, affiliation or tool you can to gain a referral or connect with someone inside your target organization. Turn cold calling into networking whenever possible to ensure the greatest chance of success.

- Ask everyone you know for an introduction to anyone who works in your target company; use all your personal networking and social media skills to connect.

- Use LinkedIn as a key source to find contacts of interest in your target company.

- Use email, snail mail and phone calls to connect with any company employee.

- Ask for referrals from company employees.

SECTION 4

GET SELECTED FOR THE INTERVIEW

Getting your résumé through the computer screening and matching process is only the first step in the hiring process. Or perhaps referrals and networking have allowed you to identify a job opening, and find the perfect job and employer.

Now you need to get invited to the interview. This requires a different set of skills, and will focus more on engaging the hiring manager than on meeting the criteria set by the recruiter or HR manager. It focuses more on soft skills than on pure credentials.

In this section, you will learn how to:

- Understand the Hiring Funnel — Chapter 22
- Get inside the head of the hiring manager — Chapter 23
- Turn your cover letter into your secret weapon — Chapter 24

22.

Understand the Hiring Funnel

According to Dr. John Sullivan, nationally recognized employment guru, in his eye-opening article "Why You Can't Get a Job — Recruiting Explained by the Numbers," finding a job is definitely a numbers game.

The average *Monster.com* job post receives around 250 applications, but it varies with top tier companies. Google, for example, receives more than one million applications per year for 4,000 job openings — so their hire rate is 4/10 of 1% (less than half of 1 percent.)

Of 1,000 people who see a job posting, only about 10% of them (100 people) will actually submit their applications. This volume of applications is still too overwhelming for a human to handle — so the preliminary screening and key word matching is done by a computer.

When you submit your application and résumé online, a computer program called ATS will probably analyze your résumé to match your qualifications to the job description by key word search.

Since 90% of applicants submit their standard résumé which has not been customized for the position being applied for, it's not surprising that 75% of applicants are rejected during the preliminary automated screening process, and only about one-quarter (25%) of résumés are seen by a human being. So it is critical that you personalize each résumé to ensure it mirrors the key words from the job description.

The Hiring Funnel

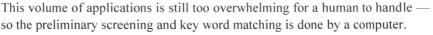

1,000 people see the job post
200 begin the application
100 submit the application
75 rejected by computer
25 seen by hiring manager
5 invited to interview
1 offered the job
80% accept

Why You Can't Get A Job ... Recruiting Explained
By The Numbers By Dr. John Sullivan, May 20, 2013 RNS

You need to carefully review all the job requirements, and only invest your time in applying for positions for which you truly match the requirements. Otherwise it's a waste of everyone's time, and you can rest assured that your résumé will be one of the 75% that get rejected before a human being ever sets eyes on it.

Of the 25% of résumés seen by the hiring manager, 4 to 6 will be selected for a live interview, 1 to 3 will be invited back for a second interview, and 1 offer will be made. In 80% of occasions, the offer will be accepted.

Understand What Will Cause Your Résumé to Be Rejected

A recruiter's most immediate challenge in reviewing résumés is to weed out all the unsuitable résumés, so he can hone in on the best candidates. This process of elimination will leave only the most qualified candidates' résumés in consideration. These statistics will help you understand the key reasons résumés are rejected, allowing you to correct many easy-to-fix errors that are proven job killers:

- 76% of hiring managers reject a résumé with a photo — even though that's what they focus on at your LinkedIn page (*BeHiring.com*)
- 61% of recruiters will reject a résumé or cover letter with a single typo (*Career Builder.com*)
- 43% of hiring managers will reject a résumé or cover letter with a single misspelling (*Adecco.com*)
- 60% or recruiters can't scan a PDF — so submit your application in Word (even if they say they accept PDF), or in both formats
- 76% of recruiters will reject your résumé for an unprofessional or inappropriate email address
- 50% of applications are rejected because the résumé did not meet the basic job requirements
- An out-of-town address can cause rejection due to fear of relocation
- Many recruiters will ignore a résumé longer than 1 page — keep it short and sweet so the high points jump out quickly
- Failure to list accomplishments will cause rejection — your performance should be quantified with numbers, volume, revenue, etc.

While finding a job is clearly a numbers game, it is one that you can play to your advantage. You now know what causes the vast majority of résumés to be rejected - now focus on what you need in your résumé so that it gets selected.

→ TAKEAWAY — Initial screening for online applications is done by a computer program that matches key words on your résumé with keywords in the job description. So only apply to jobs where you meet the exact job requirements, and personalize your résumé to the exact wording of the job requirements.

23.

Get Inside Their Heads - How Hiring Managers Select Candidates

After you have gotten though the initial computer screening and a review by the recruiter or HR manager, you may be one of the lucky 10 - 25% of candidates whose résumés will be reviewed by the hiring manager. She will assume that you have been vetted as qualified through this selection process, so her concern is more about fit than just objective qualifications.

She will be evaluating how well you fit into the company culture, the department dynamics, and how you balance the team in terms of skill set and personality. She will focus on your likeability, passion and drive, and other intangible attributes that don't show up in the hard facts on the résumé.

You need to stand out as unique, talented, personable, presentable, likeable, a team player and sharing his same values. This is the flip side of the objective computer matching of skills to requirements. List some of these desirable skills and attributes in the "Other Information" section of your résumé, where you will showcase these "soft skills" to hopefully pique the interest of the interviewer.

Job Experience and Achievements

The key criteria a hiring manager will look for is insight into what you have accomplished in your career. Your experience and achievements will be listed on your résumé in dry factual bullet format, but in an interview, you will want to tell stories about the projects you have led, initiatives you have pioneered, and other achievements you have made. During your interview, pull out your hard copy portfolio and say, *"I'd like to show you some of the exciting and successful programs I have developed."* You will come alive as you tell stories about the challenges you faced and how you overcame the problems to meet your goals. You should exude excitement, passion, dedication, intelligence, and more while you talk about your experiences. Importantly, you will become extremely memorable because of the visual stimulus of your portfolio and the power of narrative in engaging people at an emotional level.

Provide Examples of Teamwork and Leadership

Highlight and discuss roles or experiences which demonstrate teamwork and leadership. Talk about offices you have held, organizations you formed or led, volunteers you recruited, team participation achievements, and more. Potential employers see participation in organized sports very favorably because it highlights both your ability to work as part of a team while making valuable individual contributions to the success of the organization. In general, men love talking sports, so that creates camaraderie and affinity and breaks down boundaries.

Find Common Bonds to Create Affinity

You can connect at a subconscious level with your hiring decision maker through affinity. Your future boss is subconsciously looking for attributes in common and shared interests. So going to the same school, coming from the same town, belonging to the same fraternity or sorority or professional or civic association matters. Sharing a hobby, past time, sport, talent, experience, cultural background, or former employer all count in your favor.

Employers are drawn to candidates who are like them. So race, ethnicity, language, country of origin, or religion may matter at this point, at a subconscious level. If you are African American, you may want to seek out an African American hiring manager or boss, because you will have the advantage of a shared cultural bond resulting in affinity. If you are Hispanic or Asian, you may fare better working in an area or for a company where your ethnicity is an advantage, and where cultural and language skills are valuable assets for the employer.

In today's market, I don't believe any HR professional or hiring manager would ever overtly or even consciously discriminate against a candidate due to gender, race, religion, or ethnicity. But all other things equal, another candidate may be selected due to a greater affinity with the hiring manager.

Unique or Interesting Skills, Talents or Experiences to Overcome Affinity

Many other skills and talents can overcome the power of affinity. Employers are human, and they are looking for people with unique, interesting, and exciting skills and talents and experiences. You must showcase the soft skills that make you fascinating and someone the hiring manager wants to meet and talk with.

I once interviewed a young man who had worked for a leading comic book publisher, just because I wanted to talk with him and learn about his experience. I ended up hiring him because he was so interesting and provided a complementary portfolio of skills and experience. I had a student who had been a professional jockey; I would have chosen to interview him because I think it would be interesting to learn about his experiences. I have chosen to interview people because they travelled to unique places, had worked in underdeveloped countries, were professional singers, had published a book, ran a blog, and more. So showcase favorable experiences and skills in the hopes of piquing the interest of your interviewer.

→ TAKEAWAY — People hire employees who they like and with whom they form a bond. When you are past the computer screening phase and start interacting with human beings, seek out common bonds of affinity to engage the interviewer. And build captivating stories into the interview to showcase your enthusiasm and commitment, allowing you to engage at an emotional level.

24.

Turn Your Cover Letter
Into Your Secret Weapon

When you are applying for a posted job, you generally include a cover letter when you submit your résumé or job application. But only 17% of cover letters are actually read! They tend to be either fluffy summaries of the résumé, or soft information that's not relevant for the initial computer-focused screening process.

Use your cover letter as a secret weapon to stand out from all other applicants. In the letter, you simply compare your qualifications with the job requirements and mirror the language of the job posting.

Your cover letter could be something as simple as *"I'd like to apply for your XYZ job posted on Monster. I am confident that my skills and experience meet or exceed your posted job requirements."*

Then you insert a chart with the comparison — you've already done the work for them. That's all you need to say. It is self-explanatory, with no risk of confusion. It makes you the clearly logical choice for the position. Your résumé might include the same information if you personalized it for the position.

Job Requirements	My Credentials
Min. B. A. degree	B.A. in Business Administration from Texas A&M 2015
3 years experience	5+ years related work experience in Sales, Customer Service, Marketing
Excellent computer skills	Proficient in Microsoft Office Suite – Word, PowerPoint, Excel, Publisher, Access; PhotoShop; Illustrator; Quark Express; WordPress; Quickbooks

This saves the recruiter the work of manually comparing and contrasting your skills to the job requirements, ensuring that the skills match is recognized, and leaves no doubt as to whether or not you are qualified for the job.

This is a cover letter that will get read, and will be worth its weight in gold in landing you a coveted interview.

> ➡ TAKEAWAY — Your cover letter should be concise and direct, and should provide both detailed tangible information about your skills and how they match the job specifications. It may briefly describe interesting soft skills and intriguing tidbits that will cause a hiring manager to say, *"Yes, sounds like an interesting person. I'll have to meet him."*

SECTION 5

MASTER THE ART OF THE INTERVIEW

You've done it! You just received an invitation to an interview at the main office.

You are now so close to getting that offer that you can almost taste it!

Now it's time to really focus on the interview itself — because it's a whole different set of skills than those you've used to get to this point.

In this section, you will learn how to:

- Prepare for the different types and styles of interviews — Chapter 25
- Dress for success for your interview — Chapter 26
- Use research to guide you to the smart questions guaranteed to impress — Chapter 27
- Know what employers look for in your interview — Chapter 28
- Answer those 2 all-important questions — Chapter 29

25.

Understand the Interview Process and Styles of Interviews

Congratulations! The computer selected your résumé as a qualified potential candidate, and the recruiter took quality time to review your résumé and even your cover letter. Of the hundreds of people who submitted an application for the job, you have passed the first hurdles and are on your way into the interview process.

The interview process is just that — a process with multiple steps which can take several weeks or even months to complete. You need to be prepared for each step so you can move smoothly to the next round of interviews.

Each interview will be progressively more intense and personal. The company's objective is to cull the number of candidates down from perhaps 20 or 25 to the ONE right person for the job. It's not an easy decision, as there will be many good candidates with different personalities, skills and experiences. Here are some of the different types of interviews that you may experience before landing your dream job.

Telephone Screening Interview

The first step in the interview process is a call or email from a recruiter or HR employee saying they received your résumé or application and would like to conduct a brief interview on the phone at a convenient time. You will agree upon a time and date, and then the interviewer will call you on the phone at the designated time.

The initial interviewer will often be a junior HR staff person, generally not the HR manager or the hiring manager. The goal in an initial screening is to determine how well you present yourself and communicate verbally, and to verify basic employment and education details. You may be asked to submit references during this call.

This initial interview may take around fifteen minutes, and rarely will last more than half an hour. The phone interview should be scheduled in advance so you can clear your agenda and arrange to be at a quiet place where you can speak freely on a land line instead of a mobile phone — not in your office. If you take the call at home, make sure dogs are restrained or in a room where barking won't interfere with the call. If necessary, arrange for someone to take care of kids, answer the door, sign for deliveries, or handle other interruptions.

Arrange to have a mirror over or next to the phone so you can look at yourself while you are talking. When you get the visual feedback from seeing yourself speak, you will tend to speak more robustly and pleasantly, and your smile and enthusiasm will come through more clearly. Telemarketers use this trick, and it can benefit you in selling your most important product — YOU!

You will feel and act and present yourself more competently if you are dressed professionally during the phone interview. It's a subconscious thing, but you will come across better on the phone when dressed in business attire than if you are conducting the interview in your boxer shorts or bunny slippers.

Video Interview

A next step may be a video interview, scheduled through Skype for small companies, or using a conference calling platform like WebEx or GoToMeeting for larger companies. The company will send you a link to a scheduled call, possibly with a username and password. A video interview is similar to an in-person interview and will probably be conducted by a more senior executive or recruiter.

Here are tips for a successful video interview:

- You will paste the link into your browser, and it will automatically download the conference calling software onto your computer. You will need to have a good camera and microphone on your computer.
- The download process can take 5 or 10 minutes, and you could encounter problems if you have a firewall that prevents access or slow internet speed. Test out the link well before the call to make sure you won't be delayed setting up the call at the scheduled time.
- Avoid using your mobile phone for the video conference if at all possible. If you have no other option, arrange to position the phone horizontally far enough away to see your upper body, chest and head.
- Make sure you control your environment as you would for a telephone call, and make sure the wall behind you, in sight of the camera, shows a neutral or professional background.

- You may be asked to go to a location that has professional video conferencing equipment, which is expensive, but not nearly as expensive as a job interview trip.
- During this video conference, the interviewer will be able to evaluate everything that occurs in a phone interview, plus it will allow her to see what you look like, observe behavioral indicators like nervousness, tics, fidgeting, and facial expressions, and gauge how you dress and groom yourself. I have very blonde hair, and during an off-site video interview many year ago, I was asked if my hair was blonde or white — expressing subconscious concerns about my age. I replied that I was a beautiful blonde — and got the invitation to the interview at corporate headquarters.
- The video call may be recorded and shared with other people in the hiring process.
- For fun, watch _The Internship_ movie with Vince Vaugh and Owen Wilson for a look at what you should NOT do on a video interview.

In-person Interview

When you have successfully passed the phone or video interview, you may be invited for an in-person interview at a company office or headquarters. When scheduling the appointment, ask who you will be in the interviewing, so you can research them on LinkedIn before the interview. Confirm this detail the day before the interview, as the schedule should be decided by then.

The standard in-office interview starts in the HR office, where you will be greeted first by an HR employee or manager, who will speak with you for a few minutes, before conducting you to a meeting with one or more hiring managers.

The HR portion of the interview may require you to fill out and sign an application. At this point, fill in your name, contact information, Social Security number, then write _"See Résumé"_ for most sections, and sign and date the application. Your signature is key as it gives them the right to contact former employers and third parties to gather information about you. Importantly, you will be attesting that everything in the application is correct, so the company can immediately fire you without redress for misrepresenting anything on the application. You may want to attach a list of references and photocopies of rave review letters of recommendation along with your résumé.

137

Don't forget to bring 6 or more copies of your résumé on crisp bond paper, originals and copies of letters of recommendation, a list of references, and your hard copy portfolio.

The HR representative will then escort you to meet with the real decision makers — one or more hiring managers. Remember, HR will have verified your credentials by this time, so the interviews should be more personal and future-looking than the screening interviews in the past. You may encounter one of the following types of interviews:

• Sequential Interviews

You may meet back-to-back with two or three different people who work in the department you are interviewing for, and who will generally be your future supervisor or co-workers. You will spend probably 20 to 30 minutes with each person, one after another, circling back to the HR department at the end of the interview cycle. By the end of the 3 or 4 interviews, the HR manager already may have some feedback, and may ask for clarification of concerns at this point. You can ask him for feedback and how he thinks you will fit into the company.

• Panel or Committee Interview

You may find yourself interviewed by 2 to 5 people in one panel interview, where everyone can ask questions. This is a bit disconcerting, but will showcase your skills, talents and confidence in handling a more challenging interview. Respond to the person who asked a question with frequent eye contact, and look each panelist in the eye whenever possible.

• Group Interview

It is rare (I've never been in one) but you may face a group interview where several candidates are interviewed in a Panel Interview session. The interviewers may ask the group of candidates various questions, and then evaluate how each person answered. This type of interview might be used for a more senior position, or one where the employee is under pressure or scrutiny. In this type of interview, they will be judging your poise, confidence, assertiveness, temperament, leadership, and ability to take control of the questions and get your fair share of time to answer.

• <u>Formal Lunch or Dinner Interview</u>

You may be invited for a luncheon or dinner interview, especially if you are applying for a senior position, one involving travel and entertaining clients, or where social skills are important. You will be judged on your manners, etiquette, graciousness, worldliness, and likeability. Often this will be the final interview, where you will dine with a senior manager or company executive, with the objective of creating a bond between you and the interviewer and the company.

Order a moderately-priced meal, neither the cheapest nor most expensive on the menu. Ask the interviewer what he suggests, or what he's going to have, to figure out what you should order. If he orders an entrée with a soup or salad, that indicates you should order a 2-course meal so you aren't watching him eat his soup while you have nothing in front of you. An entree salad is always a good bet — it shows you are concerned with health and fitness.

 Avoid difficult-to-eat or sloppy foods like soup that can spill or spaghetti that you have to wrestle onto your fork. Drink water, tea or soda unless your interviewer orders a drink or wine. In that case you might order a glass of wine — but just one — and preferably no hard liquor. Your interviewer will be carefully watching how much you drink — heavy drinking is considered a negative trait.

If you don't have fine dining mastered, study etiquette to learn which fork and knife to use when, how to use and rest your silverware, how to place your napkin, etc. Dozens of *YouTube* videos are available to demystify fine dining; invest half an hour so you will know all the ins and outs. You might want to go to the restaurant where you will be dining and have a practice dinner (or even just soup and salad) so you feel comfortable there and know how people dress and carry themselves. It's critical that you know where the restaurant is located, and locate nearby parking or valet parking service, so you arrive at least five minutes before the agreed-upon time.

This will probably be your final interview, so make sure you invest the time and effort to master the skills to be comfortable and charming to win over the final decision maker.

• **The Fly-Back Interview**

You may be invited to travel out of town to the company's headquarters for interviews, so you will need to plan for one very intense, exciting and exhausting day. The company should provide you with a plane ticket and a voucher for transfer service to and from your hotel. You will probably fly in the evening before the interviews are scheduled. On occasion, someone may invite you to dinner that evening, but generally someone from HR will

plan to pick you up first thing in the morning on the way into the office. You should plan on having breakfast at the hotel, either on your own, or with the person who will pick you up. After arriving at the office, you will go to HR for a brief meeting, and then head to a series of scheduled interviews. You may end up in the cafeteria or executive dining room for a final meeting or interview at the end of the day before heading back to the airport.

Make sure you bring your driver's license and original Social Security card or Passport for employment verification, as you may not come back to the main office before your official hiring. Bring along at least 6 copies of your résumé, printed on fine white bond paper, a list of references for HR, copies of letters of recommendation, and your portfolio to wow them with at the interview.

The company should pay for the airfare, local transportation and hotel through direct billing. You will be asked to submit an expense report with copies of receipts for all other expenses — parking at the airport or taxi to and from the airport, checked baggage expense, meals at the airport to and from the interview (generally limited to $25 per meal), and any other customary or incidental expense, regardless of whether they offer you the job.

Interviewer Styles

In any of these types of interviews, you may encounter different interview styles. Most interviewers will be warm and friendly, asking you about your experiences, skills, background, goals, etc. But you might end up with a Stress Interview, where the interviewer is aggressive or hostile — looking to see how you handle yourself in stressful or negative situations. You may end up in a Behavioral Interview — grilled on how you would handle different hypothetical situations. You might be presented with case studies and asked what you would do. I've heard of interviews where you are given an assignment in advance and asked to bring in or submit your proposal in writing. I was once in an interview where a psychologist administered a bank of standardized personality tests and kept asking me about my relationship with my father.

Regardless of the kind of interviews you encounter, you have been selected from hundreds of candidates to come inside the company, meet the leadership team, and learn about the company, opportunity and industry. The company is investing valuable time, money and talent to screen your qualifications, conduct interviews with several employees, and arrange for your travel, meal or office visit. This means they are seriously considering you for the position, and you are on the short list for landing the job.

To be the 1 person selected, your success may well depend on 1 thing — how well you prepare for the interviews. And it does take a great deal of preparation to come out as the preferred candidate, as we will see next.

→ TAKEAWAY — The interview process is comprised of several sequential steps. Understanding what is being evaluated in each step will help you deliver what the interviewer is seeking, so you can be the one candidate selected for the job.

- Make sure your computer has a good microphone and camera for a video interview.

- Set up a mirror over your interview phone.

- Master perfect meal etiquette now by watching *YouTube* videos and practicing restaurant manners.

26.

Dress for Success

The key rule of thumb for an interview is to dress like your future boss — or your boss's boss. You can never be overdressed in an interview, but you can be underdressed. If you show up for an interview and feel overdressed, you can always remove your jacket or tie. But you can't fake it if you show up in shirtsleeves and everyone else is wearing a suit or jacket. You should already have a good interview suit you wore in your photo session. If not, invest in at least 1 or 2 good interview suits now. You'll need these when you start work anyway.

If you are interviewing for a job in the arts, music, fashion, film, high tech or other avant-garde field, the dress will probably be much more relaxed than for more conventional fields. Here's your guide to dressing for success in a traditional or conservative interview — and then later in the job itself.

<u>Attire for Men</u>

Wear a suit that is navy blue, dark grey, charcoal gray, or a black, preferably solid-colored. Wear a crisp white or pastel starched and freshly-ironed long sleeved shirt, preferably with buttoned cuffs instead of cufflinks. Your shirt cuffs should stick out ½ inch below your suit sleeve cuff when standing with your arms down by your sides. Avoid dark shirts that match the suit – it makes you look like you are in the mafia.

You need to wear a good quality silk power tie, preferably in solid colors or thin stripes or a fine pattern that ties the shirt and suit together. You can never go wrong with a red or blue power tie.

Wear polished black or dark brown shoes to match the suit, with solid black or navy blue knee-high socks so that when you cross your legs, your interviewer doesn't see three inches of hairy leg skin.

Attire for Women

Dress professionally but not sexily. For women, this generally means a professional long sleeved suit in a solid color with a white or solid colored blouse. The skirt should be knee-length or slightly longer. Avoid short skirts more than 2 inches above the knee. Your suit should generally feature a skirt, although an attractive pant suit is acceptable as well.

It doesn't need to be an expensive designer suit, but it does need to be well-cut, of quality fabric, with fine stitching, and it must fit well. In the workplace, you will need a basic navy blue suit as a staple of your wardrobe. You will be able to wear it over and over with different blouses, sweaters and accessories, so you might as well invest in it now. A basic tailored black suit will be your other wardrobe workhorse. A red suit is a power statement, and I personally think every woman should have one as well. I personally find white, beige and cream suits to be impractical as they get dirty very quickly.

Accent your suit with tasteful gold, silver or pearl earrings and perhaps a necklace or lapel pin.

You might want to avoid bracelets as they jingle and clatter when you move your hands. You can wear fashionable costume jewelry, but nothing cheap or with bling.

Wear medium height shoes with 2- or 3-inch heels. Do not hobble around in 4-inch high heels or platform shoes. You'll look silly and frivolous, not professional. Wear nude or tan hose. In the summer in the south, you can probably get away without wearing hose if you have nicely tanned legs, but it looks less professional. Avoid anything clingy or sexy — and show absolutely no cleavage. If you have to choose, look professional instead of stylish. Remember, you want to look like a no-nonsense senior female executive.

If you are in your '40s and '50s or older, you can get away with a softer look, wearing a stylish dress or softly tailored suit with appropriate accessories —but only if you are an established professional in your field. You can forego the power suit look that a younger woman relies on to look professional. However, if you are trying to reenter the workforce after years as a homemaker, go with the power look of a suit instead of a dress.

In cold climates, you may need a professional knee-length fine wool coat. No parkas or jackets please.

Tasteful Accessories

Men and women alike should have a real leather portfolio, with a pad of plain white lined paper for taking notes, and a nice soft-sided leather briefcase or attaché case. Office Depot and other office supply stores have attractive leather items at a reasonable cost. No backpacks — you don't want to look like a

college kid on campus.

You need a tasteful pen that works. It could be a Cross pen or another designer pen, which you can buy at an office supply store. You don't need a $300 Mont Blanc pen, just a nice professional-looking pen, and certainly not a cheap plastic pen from a local establishment with their logo on it.

You can bring a tablet computer to show your online portfolio, but I suggest that you not sit and take notes on the computer. It will be off-putting to an older interviewer.

Do not interact with any of your electronic devices while you're in a job interview. Put your phone on airplane mode, not just on vibrate, so you aren't interrupted when it beeps. You can't afford to be distracted or tempted to look down at your phone when a text message sounds, causing you to break eye contact with the interviewer or interrupt your train of thought. As hard as it may be to all of us who are addicted to our phones, you will find that you can live without looking at your phone for that one hour that you're going to be in the interview.

Also, be careful not to invade the interviewer's person space by plunking your purse or briefcase on the desk, creating a visual barrier. Place them on the floor by your feet or in an adjacent chair.

Ladies, I suggest you tuck a small clutch bag with key items from your purse into your briefcase so you aren't carrying multiple bags. You will need your driver's license, some cash for a vending machine perhaps, lipstick, business cards, your car key (not the whole keychain with tons of keys), some tissues and mints.

<u>Grooming to Look Your Best</u>

Make sure you look professional for your job interview. Here is a checklist to help you stay on track:

- **<u>Hair</u>**

    Men, get your hair cut about a week before the interview so it can grow out a bit before the interview. Long shaggy hair, ponytails, man-buns, and long sideburns are perceived negatively by most recruiters. Women, you should have a professional style that is easy to maintain and looks natural. You don't want to come across as high maintenance and fussy with an elaborate hairdo. No rainbow-colored hair please.

- **Makeup**

Ladies, wear discreet makeup that accentuates your best features but looks almost invisible. You want people to look at YOU, not at your makeup. Choose a natural looking foundation, light blush on upper cheekbones, natural looking eyebrow pencil and highlights, light application of liner, discreet eye shadow in gray, brown, blue or lavender — no pink please; it makes you look like you've been crying. No Goth look, no black or white lipstick or black eyeshadow.

- **Showcase Your Smile**

Make sure you have a winning smile showing a full set of teeth that are clean and shining. If your teeth are yellow, go to your dentist for a cleaning and teeth bleaching, or buy a kit from the store. Bad dental work, visible cavities, discolored or missing teeth are perceived negatively by an employer, indicating poor habits or a low-class lifestyle. You should brush and floss frequently, and make sure your gums are pink and healthy. Drink water and use mouthwash, breath mints or breath spray between interviews to make sure your breath stays fresh. Bad breath can ruin your chance of getting the job, because no one wants to work with anyone with bad breath. Smoking will be smelled on your breath, and is frowned upon, as your boss will assume you will sneak out several times during the day to smoke, resulting in lower productivity. Don't drink alcohol the day of your interview or the day before, because it can be smelled on your breath. Alcohol breath is a red flag which may indicate alcoholism, abusive drinking, absenteeism and resulting poor work behavior.

- **Nails**

Make sure your nails are nicely groomed, clean, and filed neatly; avoid bitten nails, messy cuticles or hang nails. If you have a challenge in this area, go to a nail salon and get a manicure to make sure your hands look professional. Men, this goes for you too.

Ladies, choose short to medium length nails, filed to be curved and not straight across the ends. They should be short enough so the interviewer will feel that you can type comfortably. They can be unpolished, clear polished, French manicure or polished in a discreet and attractive shade of pink, peach or red.

No decals, designs, jewels or other distractions for your nails, and no green, blue or black polish. Excessively long nails may make the interviewer think you are unable to type effectively, or that you are more concerned with glamor than functionality.

- **Facial Hair**

Men, you should be neatly shaved. Clean shaven is definitely preferred to having a beard or mustache. This is not the time for a fashionable 3-day old beard. If you wear a beard, mustache or goatee, it should be short and carefully groomed. Avoid a handlebar mustache, an unusual beard design, or anything that may make you look unprofessional, rebellious, or self-centered. If you are older and have a gray or white beard, either shave or color it because it will make you look much older and put you at a competitive disadvantage for perceived age.

- **Piercings**

If you are looking for a professional position, you should remove any body or facial piercings other than pierced earrings for the ladies. Nothing is more distracting to an interviewer than looking at a tongue ring bobbing in your mouth or hanging off your nose or lip every time you speak. In the most recent *CareerBuilder* poll, 37 percent of nearly 3,000 hiring managers said they would be less likely to promote someone with piercings. Body piercings generally indicate you are unprofessional, rebellious, and won't fit into the organization. The exception might be in the creative or arts field, or when applying for a blue-collar job, where such non-conformist appearance might be better accepted.

- **Tattoos**

Just like piercings, tattoos are generally perceived poorly by your potential employer, and probably by the recruiter as well. This is true especially for anyone seeking a professional positon, or anyone who will deal with the public. In the same *CareerBuilder* study, 31 % of HR managers said that visible tattoos can have a negative impact on their decision to hire you. You should cover any large, elaborate or counterculture tattoos, anything that indicates criminal activity including drug use, gang affiliation, or that contains profanity or nudity. A small rose delicately tattooed on a lady's ankle shouldn't be an issue; however, a tattoo impinging on your face, neck, head, or hands, which can't be covered, could substantially reduce your chances of employment. Wearing a sleeveless blouse or short sleeved shirt to show off a full sleeve of tattoos is definitely not recommended.

If you can cover visible tattoos with clothing, do so. If you can't, you can cover them with makeup or special concealers. A recent article in *US News and World Report* says you should discuss the fact that you have visible tattoos on your arms or legs with the recruiter or hiring manager, and ask if there is a dress policy that requires them to be covered at work.

➜ TAKE AWAY — Your appearance and the way you dress and groom yourself will be key factors in whether or not you get the job offer. If you want to be hired and treated as a professional, you must look, talk, and dress like one.

- Invest now in key professional attire — for men, a dark blue suit with several starched solid white or pastel shirts and a couple of coordinating fine silk ties, polished dark brown or black shoes, black or blue knee high dress socks.

- Ladies, invest in a well-tailored solid blue suit and possibly a black or red one, a couple of attractive and elegant blouses, polished shoes with 2 to 3 inch heels, solid nude or tan hose.

- Purchase an elegant soft-sided leather briefcase or attaché case, a leather portfolio, and a professional but not necessarily expensive pen.

- Make sure your grooming is impeccable — nicely groomed nails, well-cut low maintenance hair, discreet makeup, brilliant white smile and clean breath.

- Find ways to completely cover large or counterculture tattoos.

27.

Research, Research, Research — Your Key to Success

Don't ever walk into an important job interview blind. You must do your research — and a great deal of it — to be prepared to ace the interview and land the job.

Be prepared to spend between 4 and 8 hours doing research before you walk into an interview. Do not short change this if you want to get the job. Only by doing your research will you be able to ask the smart questions that will wow your interviewers.

You need to learn everything possible about the company, the position, the industry, your future boss, and more. Here's what you need to know, and how to find it:

Research Musts to Master the Interview

- Visit the company website, and read every single page. See what's new, and what their key messages are. What is their focus in the site? Pore over every page and section so you know it inside and out.

- Scroll to the very bottom of the home page, all the way down to that little, tiny type on the footer, and look for the "*Investor Relations*" link. Here is where you will find what the company is telling its shareholders. If it's a publicly traded company or a non-profit organization, you will find their financial reports and legal findings posted in this section. Read the annual report, quarterly reports, and any investor presentations from recent press briefings about the company's performance. These documents will tell you the company's financial situation, financial reports and forecasts, market information, product or brand performance, key competitors, legal issues, and more. They will give you the names of the key executives of the organization — it's a roadmap to a successful interview.

- Next, go the link or page of the website titled "*Media Relations,*" "*Press Room,*" "*Community Affairs,*" or "*Public Relations,*" or something similar. Here you will learn what they are saying to customers, retailers, and the press. It will have every press release that they've issued in the past several years, so you can see what they're talking about in the media. Read the last 10 or more press releases. What new products or services are they promoting or launching? What are the key highly visible issues that they are discussing? What are the new initiatives that they've launched? Do they have legal problems like a product recall or discrimination or trademark infringement lawsuit pending? You may find releases about promotions of top leaders and issuance of periodic financial reports.

- Study the website to see if they have links to or mention their professional or trade associations. Trade associations have a wealth of information about the industry and often the company. Go to the various trade associations for the industry and see what you can learn about the industry as a whole and the company in particular. The association may have a membership directory where you can research companies or members. See if any company employees are on the board or are key committee chairs; you may want to contact them to learn more about the industry and company, and hopefully get them to forward your résumé on your behalf, with a note to HR.

- Visit all their social media pages — *Facebook, Twitter, LinkedIn, Pinterest*, and *Google+*. See what they are promoting or discussing. Learn about social media contests so you can mention them during the interview.

- Go to *Glassdoor.com* to see what current and former employees say about them. Be aware that many people who post there or on related sites are disgruntled former employees, so look for trends and big picture issues as a red flag.

- Pore over *LinkedIn* to find profiles on everyone in the department you are applying for, and certainly for the senior managers who you might meet during the interview. When setting up the interview, ask the HR representative who will be in the interview, and confirm that information the day before the interview. Research everyone you might meet to find areas of affinity or common interests that you can exploit to create a bond.

- Research your school's alumni database to see fellow alumni who work at the company. Reach out to them in advance of the interview to ask for any suggestions they can give to make your interview more successful. See if they can give insights about upcoming programs they are working on that may not be public yet; those kinds of insights can impress your interviewer.

Be Prepared So You Can Ask Smart Questions

The goal of all this research is to be knowledgeable about the company and industry so you can ask smart questions that will impress the interviewers. Imagine the reaction when you ask insightful questions like:

- *"I understand last year was a downward year in the industry but that this company was one of only four that was able to grow revenue. What was the key factor between you and the other companies that led you to spearhead growth?"*

- *"Your company launched a major green initiative in the spring. What has been the feedback from customers and the media?"*

- *"I admired your recent Pinterest contest, and saw so many great photos posted. How do you take advantage of the database of engaged customers who participate in your contests?"*

- *"I understand you will be opening a new manufacturing plant in the Midwest in the spring. Is this due to sustained growth in existing products, or gearing up for new products or programs?"*

- *"I see that the company recently received your ISO 9000 certification. Have you seen a significant increase in quality metrics or cost reduction since that process was initiated?"*

Be prepared to knowledgably discuss what's happening in the company and the industry, not as a college student or an unemployed job candidate, but as a business peer that the interviewer wants to work with. When you demonstrate professional maturity and well-researched insight into their business, you will stand heads and shoulders above other candidates.

➡ TAKEAWAY — Detailed knowledge of the company, industry and individuals in the company can be the key to landing the job. Make sure you plan on at least 4 to 8 hours of quality online research time before an interview to be able to ask smart questions that will impress the interviewers.

- Prepare to spend 4 – 8 hours researching the company before any interview.

28.

Know What Employers Look for During an Interview

There Are Really Only 2 Reasons for an Interview

Your potential employer has already carefully reviewed your résumé, vetted your experience and credentials, and determined that you have the professional skills that the company needs. Now, they need to get to know you as a person.

There are only 2 reasons for a personal interview:

1. To see how well you present yourself and fit into the organization
2. To answer 2 key questions

Will You Fit In?

Your employer wants to know how you present yourself to judge whether you will fit into the company, the department and the team:

- Do you speak well?
- Are you neat and clean?
- Are your fingernails groomed?
- Do you dress appropriately?
- Do you shake hands firmly and talk clearly with correct grammar?
- Do you have good posture, good eye contact?
- Are you charming and personable?
- Are you relaxed and self-confident?
- Are you likeable?

This will let them know if you will fit in. They want to know:

- Are you like them?
- Are you someone that they would want to have on their team?
- Will they want to work with you on a daily basis?
- Would they be proud to have you as a colleague?

155

In the entertaining movie *The Internship*, starring Owen Wilson and Vince Vaughn, a Google employee discusses a key hiring principle — the Layover Test. Basically, if you were stuck in an airport bar during a 6-hour layover, who would you want to be stranded with? That's the person they should hire.

Likeability is key here. People don't hire people they don't like. They will hire an underqualified candidate who they like over someone who's better qualified but they don't like.

You must come across as personable and likeable. You need to be very well groomed. You need to dress like your future boss or your boss's boss. You need to present yourself well. You're there at the interview just so they can see you in action to determine if you fit with the rest of the team.

The Most Important Question — Tell Me About Yourself

You need to know how to masterfully answer the one key question that every recruiter and potential employer should ask: *"Tell me about yourself."*

And if the recruiter or interviewer doesn't ask the question, make sure you bring it up and answer it anyway.

Remember, they have already studied your résumé in great detail. They know all your credentials — where you went to school, what you studied, your GPA, where you've worked, what special skills you have.

You have to answer this question by telling them what's NOT in your résumé. They want to know what passions you have, who you are as a person, your intangible skills, your values, your work ethic, etc.

Start with the 2-Minute Drill

You should start with a well-rehearsed 2-minute drill, broken down in 5 parts:

- **Early background – 15 seconds**
  - ➢ *"I'm a Texas native, raised in San Antonio, and earned my B.A. in Marketing and my MBA from the University of Texas."*

- **Early career – 30 seconds**
  - ➤ *"I started my career with Frito-Lay in Dallas in the marketing department, and worked my way up to Product Manager of Cheetos within 4 years."*
- **Career Progress – 45 seconds**
  - ➤ *"My husband is in the Air Force, and a transfer forced me to leave that great job with Frito-Lay and move to Delaware, where I worked as the Marketing Manager for a leading pet care products company. There I managed a team of 4 professionals, and was responsible for $40 million in revenue, which we grew by 12% per year during my 3 years in that position."*
- **Transition (recent job and reason for change) – 10 seconds**
  - ➤ *"My husband has just completed his 6-year tour of duty, and we are returning to San Antonio to be near family, and happy to be back in civilian life."*
- **Why you are here today – 20 seconds**
  - ➤ *"We just got settled into our home, and I'm looking forward to taking on an exciting career challenge. I feel I am a perfect fit for your company due to your recent market advances and your forthcoming expansion into new retail distribution."*

Then Tell Them What's NOT in Your Resume – Your Personal Passions

Now share with them WHO you are, and what your values are so they know what you can contribute to the company. You should say things like:

- *"I am unflaggingly loyal to my boss and the people I work with."*
- *"I'm persuasive and have the innate ability to win people over to my point of view."*
- *"I'm a great team leader, and find myself in charge of most projects I work on."*
- *"Values and personal and professional ethics are extremely important to me."*
- *"I am so dedicated that I will go the extra mile even if I'm exhausted because I really am devoted to getting this job done."*
- *"I really love the challenges I encounter in this job, and constantly think about ways to solve them."*

You should talk about your leadership skills and how you're a natural born leader; how you contribute to your company's or organization's success; how you tackle challenges or deal with adversity; or how you use criticism to reevaluate your thinking and truly question your assumptions or biases.

When appropriate, you may want to mention occasions that show your grit, determination, or resilience. Talk about how you've overcome challenges and what you learned from the experience. So you might say something like, *"My dad died when I was twelve years old and I had three younger brothers, so I took the responsibility of helping to raise them. I had to learn great organizational skills to try*  and manage three young children when I was really a child myself, and even worse, three teenagers as we all got a few years older. But what it taught me was how important communication and organization skills are."* I'd want to hire you after hearing that!

Talking about a bad car accident or a debilitating disease and how you battled to overcome it shows backbone and grit which most employers will value. If you worked to support yourself through school, that's a positive trait to showcase. Employers want to know your character, values, drive and commitment, so you should highlight those attributes in a job interview.

A New York Times Bestseller by Angela Duckworth is called *"Grit: The Power of Passion and Perseverance."* This is popular in business circles, so "grit" is a word you might use in an interview to demonstrate you are keeping up with key industry trends.

Know How to Answer the WHY Question

The other key question you need to answer masterfully is WHY. Each person has a different WHY. What is your WHY?

- *"Why do you want to work for us?"*
- *"Why do you want to work in this field?"*
- *"Why did you choose this career?"*

The answer to the WHY question can make or break your interview. What you DON'T want to say is all the tangible stuff:

- *"I hear sales jobs pay well."*
- *"I started as an engineering major but I flunked out of calculus so I ended up in the business school because it was easier."*
- *"I had to choose a major so I thought this was kind of interesting."*
- *"I need a job when I graduate."*
- *"No one else is hiring."*

Those answers are NOT going to get you the job.

You should talk about your passions instead. Tell them WHY they should want you on their team. Share statements like:

- *"I want to work in Customer Service because I absolutely love helping people."*
- *"I enjoy understanding consumer motivation and desire and trying to figure out why people do what they do."*
- *"I'm passionate about creating new ideas and new businesses and taking them to completion."*
- *"I enjoy working with a team and building something wonderful together."*
- *"I thrive on the challenge of taking on a big project and breaking it down into small steps and then making it easy to accomplish."*
- *"I believe many low-income seniors aren't getting adequate health care, so I am dedicated to make sure they have access to good doctors and medicine they can afford."*

That's the WHY they want to hear.

But you must be honest. Don't just make up what you think they want to hear. This has to come from your heart or it will come out as phony.

Even worse, if you get the job, you won't be happy, and neither will your employer, if they hired you based on passions and intentions you don't really have. The WHY has to be honest because otherwise you're wasting your time and theirs, and you shouldn't be in that job if you don't have passion for it. Find another job that you're passionate about. That's why earlier in the book we focused on self-examination to identify your likes, dislikes, strengths and weaknesses. Those insights should guide you throughout your job search., and help you communicate your WHY.

→ TAKEAWAY — A face-to-face interview has just two purposes — to see how you present yourself in person, and to learn how you answer the Tell Me About Yourself question by explaining your WHY.

- Master your 2-minute drill to keep your background presentation short and sweet.

- Prepare answers to the "Tell Me About Yourself" question that showcase your intellect, drive, commitment, passion, grit and values.

- Prepare and memorize your WHY – to talk about your motivation.

29.

Ask Smart Questions
to Impress Your Interviewer

During the interview, you should ask intelligent, probing questions about your specific job that will show how interested you are in the company and how you can contribute. Remember, it's all about them, not about you.

Identify Their Pain to be Able to Offer Solutions

One smart strategy is to try and identify their challenges and pain points so you know where you can best be of value. Use the research you did to comment on possible problems in the company. You may also ask questions that demonstrate your empathy, such as:

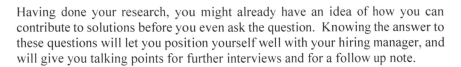

- *"What are the 3 biggest problems that you've been facing?"*
- *"What are the key problems that keep you up at night?"*
- *"If I started in this job tomorrow, what would be the key way that I could make your life easier?"*
- *"What could I do to contribute to this department tomorrow to solve a problem that you have?"*

Having done your research, you might already have an idea of how you can contribute to solutions before you even ask the question. Knowing the answer to these questions will let you position yourself well with your hiring manager, and will give you talking points for further interviews and for a follow up note.

Is This the Right Job for You?

Ask questions to learn whether or not you will fit into the company culture and like the job and the people you will work with:

- *"How would you describe the company's culture?"*
- *"What was it that attracted you personally to come and work for this company?"*
- *"What have you found to be your most fulfilling accomplishment in the years that you've worked for this company?"*

161

Show that you're really interested in understanding the company culture — they will see if as a favorable expression of sincere interest and you will learn more about the company.

Look for the Interview Shift — When They Start Selling YOU on the Job

During the first part of the interview, they will be asking you questions to decide whether or not they want to hire you. A successful interview is when a subtle shift happens — the interviewer starts selling YOU on the company. Instead of asking you questions, the interviewer will tell you how great the company is, tell you about benefit plans, events the company hosts, holiday celebrations, rewards and referral programs, etc. This is a great signal that you have passed the key hurdles and will be on the short list for either a call back interview or a job offer. This is a great time to start asking the *"How can I contribute"* smart questions.

Ask for Feedback Before You Leave

Make sure you learn how you were perceived by the interviewers before you leave, so you have realistic expectations and can learn from the experience to be better at the next interview. As the time with each interviewer winds down, you should ask something like, *"I've really enjoyed speaking with you and learning about the company and this position. I'd like to know if you think I'm a fit for the job, or if you have any concerns about me in this role."* Then listen carefully to the response. Ask a follow-up question to clarify the feedback if necessary. This gives you the opportunity to learn more about the company and the job expectations, and to clarify any misinterpretations or doubts the interviewer may have.

Find Out When the Decision Will Be Made

This is the perfect time for you to ask *"When do you expect to make a decision about this position?"* It will give you an idea of how far along they are in the decision-making process. This gives you the opportunity to say, *"Friday morning? That's great. I'll give you a call around noon if I don't hear from you by then."* It shows you are serious about the position. Then follow up at noon exactly on Friday.

What NOT to Ask

Don't ask a hiring manager about salary or benefits — save that for discussion with HR only. Talk with the hiring manager about the job responsibilities, not the benefits.

And when you do ask HR about money, ask about compensation and benefits instead of salary. You can say, *"If I am selected for this positon, what kind of compensation package could I expect?"* Don't push the salary topic at this stage. It's a moot point until you get an offer, so focus on other job-related issues to sell your case to the hiring team. Remember, at this point it's about the company and meeting their needs, not about meeting your needs. The rest will come later when you are selected for the position.

→ TAKEAWAY — To ace the interview, you need to thoroughly research the company and the people you will meet, so you can ask smart insightful questions that will wow the interviewer. When you present yourself professionally and exude confidence, you have a great chance of success.

- Use your research to formulate smart questions for the hiring manager that show your commitment.

- Look for the interview shift — when they start selling you instead of you selling them.

- Always ask for feedback before leaving each interview.

SECTION 6

GETTING AND ACCEPTING THE OFFER

Congratulations, you made it through the interview!

Now, you are waiting eagerly to see if you are offered the job. While the decision is mainly in the hands of the company, you've still got lots of work to do before you close the deal!

In this final Section, you will learn how to:

- Follow up the interview to remain top of mind — Chapter 30
- Gracefully receive and negotiate the best possible offer — Chapter 31
- PLUS - Last thoughts on the job-hunting process — Chapter 32

30.

Follow up the Interview
to Remain Top of Mind

Data released by *CareerBuilder* shows that hiring managers are more likely to hire a job candidate who sends a thank you note after the interview. They feel it shows real interest in the job, and demonstrates your thoroughness and follow up ability.

According to Amanda Augustine, job search expert for *TheLadders.com*, *"Based on my decade-long experience in conducting interviews, I can attest first-hand that failure to follow-up can be the deciding factor in rejecting a candidate who is otherwise a great fit."*

Email a Thank You Note Immediately

Immediately after the interview, send an email to each person your met or interviewed with, thanking them for their time and interest, and reiterating your interest in the job. Send the email the same day as the interview, or no later than noon the next day. You can mention how you hope to contribute to helping the company meet its goals, using the insights you gained from speaking with so many people during the interviews.

Make sure you get a business card from each person you meet during the interview, so that you can appropriately address the email thank you note.

An *Accountemps* survey indicates that 87% of hiring managers now view email as an appropriate way to express thanks after a job interview. Find sample email templates at BrandYouGuide.com.

Send a Hand-written Follow-Up Note

At the same time, immediately write and mail a handwritten or typed note to each person you met at the interview. According to one source, as many as 25% of hiring managers say they wouldn't hire someone who didn't send a post-interview thank you letter. The key is to send it immediately, no less than 24 hours after the interview.

167

It's not overkill to send both the email and a hard copy thank you note. The written note will arrive several days after the email, reminding them of you and keeping your name top of mind. Find sample thank you letter templates at BrandYouGuide.com.

Call the HR Manager When the Decision is Due — If They Don't Call You First

When you leave HR after the final interview, they will tell you when the decision should be made. You should agree when you will call to learn about the final decision. Then call them when you said you would. Set a reminder on your phone and calendar so you call at exactly the agreed-upon time. Hopefully they will call you beforehand, but plan on this contingency anyway.

➔ TAKEAWAY — Immediately follow up your interview with both an email and a hard-copy thank you letter to everyone you met on the interview. And follow up professionally by phone and email with the HR manager until you either receive your offer or are advised that they have selected another candidate.

To Do List

- Immediately email a thank you note to everyone your met during the interview process the same day.

- Hand write and mail and thank you not to everyone you interviewed with.

- Ask HR when decision is due — and follow up at the specified time.

31.

Negotiate Your Job Like a Pro

Receiving the Offer

You will generally receive the job offer via a phone call from the HR Manager, congratulating you on being selected for the position, and presenting the details of the offer.

Once the hiring decision has been made, it is the responsibility of HR to sell you on the position, offer and compensation. HR will try to convince you about the benefits of the job, the company, and the salary. Its HR's responsibility to get you to agree to work for the company once the hiring decision has been made. The decision to make you the offer has been made, and now it is HR's responsibility to close the deal and get you to sign on the dotted line.

The call will go something like, *"Hello, Roberta. I'm pleased to say that we'd like to offer you this position."* The HR representative will detail the title of the position, who you will report to or what department the position is in, expected travel or relocation, your base salary, any bonus or commission potential, and the benefits package. She will explain vacation and holiday policies, and any waiting periods, such as a probation period or the customary 30 to 90 days waiting period before you will become eligible for group medical insurance.

At this point, you are jumping for joy and want to scream *"YES! YES!"* Instead, you should say, *"Thank you very much. I'm very pleased, and I look forward to working with your company. When do you need a decision?"* You don't accept the offer right then.

That's because you want time to negotiate the best possible offer.

Negotiating Salary

The company has an approved salary range for the position, and they're going to offer you the lowest price to see if you will take it. If so, they have saved the company money while hiring the desired candidate.

The initial offer may be something like, *"For this position, the salary is $32,000 a year."*

Now you will want to respond with, *"I'm very pleased with the position and the opportunity to work with the company and with Betty* (who you just learned will be your direct supervisor.) *However, I was really looking for a base salary of $36,500 to be competitive with local industry standards for this position."* Make sure you have already researched industry salaries in your market using resources like *Glassdoor* which publishes salary surveys so your expectations are realistic.

Whatever they offer, ask for 10% - 15% more.

The HR manager might respond with *"The highest we could go would be $34,000 for this level."* Bingo! You just received $2,000 more than they offered, and you look like a professional. You're talking with her, negotiating, and discussing alternatives.

Next, ask, *"Is there any way we could make it a flat $35,000? I think that would be fair, and it will recognize the fact that I will complete my MBA in four months."* Give a reason to concede. If she says *"Absolutely not, $34,000 is the firm cap for the position,"* move on to negotiate other items.

The HR manager may be able to agree to the requested salary on the spot, or she may ask to get back with you shortly. Either way, wait until you get confirmation of salary before continuing to discuss the other benefits.

TIP — Negotiate Based on Your Skills, Not Your Needs
Negotiate your salary based on industry standards, documented salary averages, merits of your work, skills you bring to the table, or past or expected contributions. Do NOT negotiate on your personal needs, or say things like, *"I need more money because my kids will start college soon,"* or *"I need a higher salary because I am building a new house."* Those are your problems or challenges, not the company's. You will be hired and paid based on your perceived contribution to the company, and for your market value. Period.

Negotiate Non-Salary Compensation

Once you receive confirmation of your salary, don't stop there. Now's the time to ask for additional non-salary items that will contribute to your full compensation package. You might ask the following questions:

- *"Is there a signing bonus available?"*
- *"You say I will receive a review after 12 months to be eligible for a raise. Could we schedule it for 6 months instead?"* The goal is to accelerate your raise by 6 months which will result in higher earnings over the life of your career.
- *"Are there performance bonuses available at this level?"*
- *"Do you have a stock option plan that I could be eligible for?"*
- *"Does this position pay overtime?"* New rules may require overtime pay for anyone earning less than $47,476 per year, so if you are close to this amount, you might be able to negotiate a salary above that minimum to avoid the overtime regulation.

These questions will indicate that you are a skilled and experienced negotiator, and are working at a professional level. If you don't ask, they may not be offered. You have nothing to lose and everything to gain by asking for additional compensation options at this time.

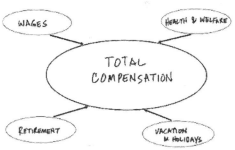

Negotiate Working Conditions

The workplace is changing, and many companies offer different working accommodations to lure quality employees. Don't assume you need to go to an office every day from 8 to 5. There may be options that you will find more satisfying and will enhance your work satisfaction.

- **Work Remotely** — Some companies will let you work from a home office either full time or part time, depending on the position. Since many companies provide laptops linked to the company portal, you can work anywhere anytime. Ask if this is available. Working at home just one or optimally two days a week can save you hundreds or thousands of dollars in auto expenses, parking and lunches out. Research has shown it provides significant productivity increases and reduced costs for the employer. So explore this option while negotiating your work conditions.

- **Flex Time** — Ask if you can work flexible hours to make commute times easier, or ease your child care responsibilities, if appropriate.

- **Equipment Provided** — Find out if the company will provide you with a laptop or mobile phone. Employees who work from a home office often receive a printer/scanner/fax machine, and payment for home high speed internet service and a phone line for the fax machine. This benefit can be worth thousands.

- **Company Credit Card or Travel Card** — Depending on your position, you may be eligible for a company credit card to avoid having to pay for travel and miscellaneous business expenses with personal funds, and then wait for reimbursement. Check on this if you will incur these expenses.

- **Specialized Training** — Companies often offer extensive training for employees, so if you have a goal of gaining expertise or a certification in a special field, your company may be willing to pay for it. Perhaps your employer will pay for you to gain your PMP (Project Management Professional) certification, or pay for your CPA exam and refresher classes, or provide a Negotiating Skills seminar. Such training is part of the company's talent acquisition and development program, and will help you develop skills you will use on the job to the company's benefit.

- **Tuition Reimbursement** — Many companies offer tuition reimbursement for college degree programs, up to a certain cost each year. They frequently come with a vesting period which requires you to work for the company for a period of a year or two after payment, or you will need to refund the tuition paid on your behalf. You may also be required to pass the class with a B or C. But this single benefit can be worth tens of thousands of dollars. Ask now to know if this is possible. If you have finished your undergraduate degree, take advantage of this benefit to start on a Master's Degree paid for by your employer.

- **Job Start Date** — Agree upon the day you will start work, generally within 2 weeks of accepting the offer, and definitely no later than 4 weeks. This gives you time to provide a 2-week notice to your current employer, have a few days to take care of personal tasks, and maybe take a quick vacation before plunging into the challenge of the new job. Your new boss will want you to start right away, so balance your needs with those of the company to set a firm start date. If by chance your current employer says you can leave before the 2-week notice is over, it is fine to let HR know that you can start earlier if you wish. But don't ask to extend the start date later if at all possible.

Lastly, Negotiate Other Benefits

Once you've agreed on the salary and working conditions, it's time to get the maximum benefits possible. Some benefits are negotiable, while others are not, often because of union contracts, legal regulations, or company policy. You have nothing to lose, and much to gain, so ask for concessions if they are important to you.

- **Timing of Medical Waiting Period** — Waiving the waiting period for group medical insurance may be one thing to ask for, and your HR contact will let you know if it is possible, or if it is tied to a specific contract that prevents changes. COBRA rates from your prior job are probably much higher than your new company's subsidized rates, so changing the eligibility date could save you thousands of dollars.

- **Vacation** — You should definitely try to negotiate more vacation time, especially if you are a seasoned professional with more than 5 or 10 years of experience. Many companies have outdated time-off policies, in which you get just 2 weeks of paid vacation after 1 year of service, and then 3 weeks of vacation for 5-10 years of service, and then 4 weeks for more than 10 years with the same company. At a minimum, you should ask for the same amount of vacation as any person in a similar position or with the same amount of work experience. So, if you worked for 10 years for various companies to gain the credentials to become the Manager of Customer Service, then you should ask for 4 weeks of paid vacation commensurate with your 10 years of experience.

Negotiate Special Treatment or Conditions Before Accepting the Job

If you need to have extra personal time off during the first year, negotiate it at this time. Many companies require you to work for at least six months and accrue vacation before you can take any time off. So, if you are going to be the best man at your brother's wedding in another state, or you have plans to attend a family reunion, or you have scheduled a trip for your wedding anniversary, discuss it now to make sure in advance that you can take that vacation time, and whether it will be paid or unpaid. After you have been hired, it is very difficult to negotiate this kind of exception during your first year of employment.

This is also the time to gain permission to leave work early to attend classes. You might say *"I'm getting my MBA at XYZ school, and this semester I have to be in classes on Saturdays, and I have a 5 PM class two nights a week. So I need to leave the office by 4:15 on Tuesdays and Thursdays. Would it be possible to*

come in early those days, or make up the time by working late on other days?"
You should have no problems getting agreement when you negotiate it up front
and it becomes a condition of employment.

Work Out the Details with HR, Not Your Boss

All of these details should be negotiated with HR, and not with your future boss,
as soon as the salary has been agreed upon. Your hiring manager just wants you
to show up for work as soon as
possible.

Once you have agreed with the HR
manager on the salary, benefits, and
terms of employment, ask her to send
the detailed or revised proposal to you
in an email for review. This should take
less than a day.

Gracefully Accept the Offer

You should have had time to think about the offer as the HR manager was
clarifying what she could and could not offer you. So shortly after receiving the
detailed offer, call her back and graciously accept (or potentially reject) the offer
so the company is not left stranded.

➜ TAKEAWAY — Never accept the first salary offered — ask for 15% more.
Negotiate the details of the offer, starting with salary, bonuses or additional non-
salary compensation, working conditions, benefits, and lastly, special
circumstances or exceptions.

Congratulations! You've just landed your dream job!

32.

Now You're on Your Way to Success

If you've gotten this far, then you have learned all the secrets to brand yourself to find and land your dream job.

Follow this step-by-step guide, and you should be able to secure a great job in just a couple of months.

Your job search is a process, and not a particularly fast or easy one. But now you have all the tools and insights you need to find a great job opening, respond effectively to an online posting, send an effective cold call letter to the employer, and network your way to success.

When you become one of the handful of prospects selected for an interview, you can now comfortably go to that interview confident that you have the skills and knowledge to "wow" the interviewers.

And now you know how to negotiate the best possible compensation package like a pro, so you can be confident you are valued and earning what you are worth in the marketplace.

Best of luck on finding and landing your dream job!

RESOURCES TO HELP YOU ON
THE PATH TO SUCCESS

Brand You Guide — www.BrandYouGuide.com
Here you will find free templates, checklists, examples, resources, and so much more. You can take advantage of our low-cost services to write or enhance your résumé, build your LinkedIn page, create an effective cover letter, write a press release, create your business card and visual branding, build your website, or benefit from one-on-one coaching. Register to receive our newsletter or subscribe to our blog. Use coupon code BU25 to receive a 25% discount off your first purchase.

VistaPrint — www.VistaPrint.com
This is a great source for all your printing needs. Take advantage of their easy-to-use templates to create your powerful and memorable business card to establish your personal brand. Additionally, they offer affordable personalized note cards, letterheads and envelopes. You can also print low-cost business cards and letterheads at quick print shops like The UPS Store, FedEx Office AKA Kinkos, or office supply stores like Office Depot and Staples.

Job Search Sites
There are dozens of websites which offer job listings and online applications. Many will archive your resume for ease of submission, and allow you to track applications. Almost all have published research studies, and have a wealth of statistics, insights, tips and services which can help you in your job search. Here are some of the most highly recommended:

- LinkedIn
- CareerBuilder
- Monster
- Indeed
- Job.com
- TheLadders
- Robert Half
- Glassdoor
- JobMo
- US.jobs
- SimplyHired
- SWITCH app
- JobR app
- JobCase

Social and Digital Media Sites
Claim you name by registering for a free account at all these free social media and digital branding sites immediately. You don't need to build out a page right now, but make sure you secure you professional name before someone else claims it:

- LinkedIn
- Google+
- Twitter
- Pinterest
- YouTube
- Instagram
- SnapChat

Tools to Manage Your Online Presence

These sites can help manage your online presence and professional reputation:

- Godaddy
- Skype
- MailChimp
- EventBrite
- Knowem
- Namech_k
- Hootsuite
- Dashlane
- Google Alert

Email Management Tools and Tracking Services

Learn when someone opens your email by using one of these services that were the top ranked by *Computer World* in 2015:

- Gmail
- Wisestamp
- Bananatag
- Boomerang
- Mail2Cloud
- MailTrack
- Sidekick
- YesWare

National Photo Studio Chains for Corporate Portrait

Get a great professional photo for all your job-hunting needs at a local photo studio, or one of these national chains:

- Picture People
- Target
- Olan Mills
- Glamour Shots
- Penny's
- LifeTouch

Online Portfolio Services

Your university may offer online portfolio hosting for free. A number of companies offer free or low cost online portfolio hosting. Try some of these well-regarded companies:

- Pathbrite
- Issuu
- Carbonmade
- DROPR
- Cargo Collective
- Behance.net
- Coroflot

Press Release Distribution Sites

The largest and most prestigious press release sites include PR Newswire and Business Wire, but their services can be expensive. To receive free or inexpensive press release distribution, try some of these sites:

- Google News — http://Googlenewssubmit.com/ currently $19
- PR.com — http://www.pr.com/
- Online PR News — https://www.onlineprnews.com/
- PressReleaser.org — http://pressreleaser.org/
- Open PR — http://www.openpr.com/news/submit.html

BIBLIOGRAPHY, SOURCES, CITATIONS, OPINIONS AND MORE

All opinions and insights presented in this book are my own unless attributed otherwise.

The workplace today is gender-neutral, so I refer to people as *"he"* or *"she"*, and no meaning should be attributed to the pronoun choice.

In writing this book, I did not consult, read or research any other books about this topic. I relied on my own experience garnered over more than 3 decades in the business world, having interviewed hundreds of candidates, and employing many dozens of people.

I did, however, conduct extensive online research on specific topics and gained valuable insights on the most current job statistics and market trends.

In today's digital world, information is openly shared across multimedia platforms, and an enormous amount of information is freely available through Google and other online search platforms. I found that the majority of relevant information was made available by companies engaged in the job search and recruiting industry, via their websites, blogs and white papers. Few provided dates of publication or author attribution. In this fluid environment, many documents cited each other, so identifying original sources was sometimes a challenge.

Here are some key sources of information I found of value in learning about the job search and recruiting market, and which can benefit any job seeker:

<u>Works Cited</u>

"50 Job Search Statistics Successful Job Seekers Need To Know"
Julliengordon.com, 11 Feb. 2013

"50 HR and Recruiting Statistics For 2016" - *glassdoor.com*/ b2b-Assets

"8 Useful Recruitment Infographics | *Recruiterbox Blog*

Adler, Lou. "This Single Job Hunting Statistic Will Blow Your Mind" -
LinkedIn.com, The Adler Group, 28 June 2016

"All Your Tricky Questions About Job Hunting On The Job" - *Forbes.com*,
The Muse, 15 Aug. 2015

"Average Salaries by Job and U.S. Location" - *Simply Hired.com*

"Best Internships For College Students" - *Experience.com*

"Career Statistics:" - *Experience.com*

Dahlstrom, Harry. *Turn a Job Fair into a Job Offer*. Holliston, MA, Dahlstrom Company, 2009

"Dr. John Sullivan - Article Archive | ERE Media." *EREMedia.com*

Economy, Peter. "11 Interesting Hiring Statistics You Should Know | Inc.com." - *Inc.com*

"HR Statistics and Best Practices | Glassdoor.com." - *GlassDoor.com*

"Job Seekers Archives | *Simply Hired Blog*."

McDonald, Paul. "Robert Half Blog - Advice to Find a Job." *Roberthalf.com/Blog*, 4 Nov. 2016

"Millennial College Graduates: Young, Educated, Jobless." *Inc.com*, 5 June 2015

"NCES Fast Facts - National Center for Education Statistics." Sources: U. S. Department of Education, National Center for Education Statistics, (2016), The Condition of Education 2016 (NCES 2016-144), Employment Rates and Unemployment Rates by Educational Attainment,

"Official LinkedIn Blog." *LinkedIn.com*

"Seven Mistakes to Avoid When Job Hunting - Forbes." *Forbes.com*, 16 July 2015

Sicola, Laura. "Want to Sound Like a Leader? Start by Saying Your Name Right." TEDx PENN, TEDx Talks; video published 4 June, 2014

Sportelli, Natalie. "Congrats On Graduating, Class of 2016! Here's What You Need to Know About the Real World", *Forbes.com*, 4 May 2016

Sullivan, Dr. John. "Why You Can't Get A Job ... Recruiting Explained By the Numbers" - *www.eremedia.com*, 20 May 2013

"The Class of 2015 - Economic Policy Institute." *Epi.org*, Economic Policy Institute

"The Ultimate List of Hiring Statistics - LinkedIn." *LinkedIn.com*

Modern Language Association 8th edition formatting by BibMe.org.

THANKS TO MY EDITORS

Deep thanks go out to three wonderful friends who took their time to painstakingly read, edit and suggest revisions to the manuscript:

- Career coach, founder of Executeam SW Business Consulting, and franchising guru Brook Carey of Schertz TX

- Fellow T-Bird alumni and non-profit leader Carla Schworer of Las Vegas NV

Emily Groenner, University Business Communication Instructor and Career Counselor, St. Cloud MN

ABOUT NAMES USED IN THIS BOOK

All names and contact information for sample business cards, résumés, elevator pitches and scripts in this book are taken from real people I know, but modified to protect their privacy. With hundreds of millions of people, phone numbers and addresses in this country, it is possible that someone does have an email or phone number or address that I made up. However, it is coincidental. If it is your name, email, phone number or address, please accept my apologies for any inconvenience it may cause you.

IMAGE LICENSES

Most images used in this book were licensed from Dreamstime.com, or are proprietary images created especially for this book. Logos of recommended sites were sourced online from the respective sites. If you feel any images were used inappropriately or without permission, please contact me immediately at Diane@BrandYouGuide.com so they can be removed.

INDEX

MEET THE AUTHOR

I'm Diane Huth, and I love helping other people achieve their goals.

I've worked in marketing forever (more than 30 years — yikes!) and I have loved at least 95% of everything I've done. I've run larger marketing departments for companies like Johnson & Johnson and Mission Foods, and worked in smaller entrepreneurial companies like Skinny Snacks and Biovideo.

I've screened thousands of résumés, interviewed hundreds of job candidates, hired scores of employees, and have mentored at least thirty college interns.

I am currently the CMO (Chief Marketing Officer) for Biovideo, a company that films the most heartwarming moments of a baby's first day, and transforms the images into a breathtaking video that we give to new parents at their baby's birth. So my day job lets me gift happiness all day long! Check it out at www.Biovideo.com or our Facebook Page at www.facebook.com/MyBiovideo.

For more than ten years I've been a Senior Innovation Strategist for Prodigy Works, creating breakthrough new product and innovation programs for leading national brands and companies.

Recently, I started teaching marketing and branding to college students at 3 different universities in my spare time, and I was shocked to learn how unprepared they were for their upcoming job search. These students had just spent 4 years of their young lives, and often $100,000 or more on college tuition, and they had no idea how to find a job when they graduated. So I wrote this book to help them — and you — find and land your dream job.

I currently teach part time at Texas A&M University and The University of the Incarnate Word, both in San Antonio, and I thank my great students for letting me try out and fine tune the content of this book.

I am now embarking on what I consider to be my life's work — making the field of marketing fun and easy to understand.

I recently realized that everything you need to know about marketing you can learn from a superhero. Things like a unique superpower is your competitive advantage, the importance of a captivating story, dedication to a noble mission, the importance of a memorable name, the overarching need for a powerful logo, strong visual identity, flair and pizzazz, archenemies as competitors and Gotham City as your marketplace, and so much more. I am now writing that book in sections, and you will be able to find out more about it when you visit www.SuperheroBranding.com. I expect to publish that work in mid-2017.

**SUPERHERO
BRANDING**

In the rest of my spare time, I live in San Antonio Texas, but with an eye on retiring to a white sandy beach in Mexico soon. But I plan many trips to Vancouver, Washington to see my only son Alex who lives there with his wife Rachel and hopefully a bunch of redheaded grandchildren in a few years.

Contact me at Diane@BrandYouGuide.com or visit my website at www.BrandYouGuide.com. And look for me on Facebook and Pinterest!

Please email me and let me know how your job search turned out, and what you found most helpful from reading this book. And let me know if I left out anything you urgently need to know – I'll add it to an update soon.

BEFORE YOU GO...

If you enjoyed this book and found it to be valuable, please take just one more minute to write a brief review for Amazon, and hopefully give it a 5-star rating.

It will give me feedback, and help others in their journey to land their dream job as well.

Thanks so much for your help!

Diane Huth

Made in the USA
Middletown, DE
10 April 2017